Routledge Revivals

England's Ideal

Originally published in 1887, Edward Carpenter's *England's Ideal and other Papers on Social Subjects* is a collection of his essays in the field of social science with a focus on English society at the time of writing. His writing was so influential that there was a near constant demand in the late nineteenth and early twentieth centuries for this work to be reprinted with this particular edition being published in 1919. Papers included in this volume discuss issues such as labour, trade and property and all provide insight into the English class structure as well as illuminating Carpenter's socialist values. This title will be of interest to students of sociology.

England's Ideal
And Other Papers on Social Subjects

Edward Carpenter

First published in 1887
by George Allen & Unwin Ltd

This edition first published in 2016 by Routledge
2 Park Square, Milton Park, Abingdon, Oxon, OX14 4RN
and by Routledge
711 Third Avenue, New York, NY 10017

Routledge is an imprint of the Taylor & Francis Group, an informa business

© 1887 George Allen & Unwin Ltd

All rights reserved. No part of this book may be reprinted or reproduced or utilised in any form or by any electronic, mechanical, or other means, now known or hereafter invented, including photocopying and recording, or in any information storage or retrieval system, without permission in writing from the publishers.

Publisher's Note
The publisher has gone to great lengths to ensure the quality of this reprint but points out that some imperfections in the original copies may be apparent.

Disclaimer
The publisher has made every effort to trace copyright holders and welcomes correspondence from those they have been unable to contact.

A Library of Congress record exists under LC control number: 96206109

ISBN 13: 978-1-138-18448-0 (hbk)
ISBN 13: 978-1-315-64514-8 (ebk)
ISBN 13: 978-1-138-18449-7 (pbk)

ENGLAND'S IDEAL

SOME OPINIONS OF THE PRESS.

CONTENTS: England's Ideal—Modern Money Lending and the Meaning of Dividends—Social Progress and Individual Effort—Desirable Mansions—Simplification of Life—Does it Pay?—Trade—Private Property—The Enchanted Thicket.

This is a volume of the *Social Science Series*. On its first appearance it attracted considerable attention, and there has been a steady demand for it ever since.

"There is something in these papers to remind the reader of Ruskin, something to remind him of Walt Whitman, and more to remind him of Thoreau. But they are far from being echoes of the thoughts of any of these men, or of anyone else. Mr. Carpenter is at least an original inquirer and thinker, and as such he stimulates thought in others. This service of making them think is the highest service a writer can do for his fellow-men and women."—*Academy*.

"The author of this book knows well how to express his ideas; indeed, to him writing, we should think, is a pleasant occupation—a recreation rather than the toil it is to most people. The result is that he has a fresh and lively style, and that the reader gets interested in what he has to say."—*Inquirer*.

"These essays should have been got up luxuriously, and offered at half a guinea, for they are specially addressed to the rich. Their literary power is unmistakable, their freshness of style, their humour, and their amiable enthusiasm."—*Pall Mall Gazette*.

"A clear, candid, gentle mind looks out from every page, and those who disagree with the author's views will be the better for coming into contact with the author's spirit."—*National Reformer*.

ENGLAND'S IDEAL

and OTHER PAPERS ON SOCIAL SUBJECTS

BY

EDWARD CARPENTER

LONDON: GEORGE ALLEN & UNWIN LTD.
NEW YORK: CHARLES SCRIBNER'S SONS

First Edition, *June* 1887; Second Edition, *February* 1895;
Third Edition, *June* 1901; Fourth Edition, *September* 1902;
Fifth Edition, *February* 1906; Sixth Edition, *June* 1909;
Seventh Edition, *December* 1913; Eighth Edition,
February 1917; Ninth Edition, *March* 1919.

CONTENTS

	PAGE
ENGLAND'S IDEAL: Reprinted from "To-Day," May, 1884	1
MODERN MONEY-LENDING, AND THE MEANING OF DIVIDENDS: A Tract for the Wealthy	23
SOCIAL PROGRESS AND INDIVIDUAL EFFORT: A Lecture given at Sheffield, February, 1885	55
DESIRABLE MANSIONS: Reprinted from "Progress," June, 1883	75
SIMPLIFICATION OF LIFE: A Paper read before the Fellowship of the New Life, January, 1886	95
DOES IT PAY? Reprinted from "To-Day," October, 1886	121
TRADE: Reprinted from "To-Day," January, 1887	128
PRIVATE PROPERTY: A Lecture given in London and in Edinburgh, 1886	139
THE ENCHANTED THICKET: An Appeal to the "Well-to-Do"	166

ENGLAND'S IDEAL.

"Behold the hire of the laborers, . . . which is of you kept back by fraud, crieth : and the cries of them . . . are entered into the ears of the Lord of Sabaoth."

WHILE it seems to be admitted now on all hands that the social condition of this country is about as bad as it can be, and while many schemes, more or less philanthropic or revolutionary, are proposed for its regeneration, it just occurs to me to bring forward, by way of balance, the importance of personal actions and ideals. For as the nation is composed of individuals, so the forces which move the individual— the motives, the ideals, which he has in his mind— are, it seems to me, the main factors in any nation's progress, and the things which ultimately decide the direction of its movement.

At the bottom, and behind all the elaborations of economic science, theories of social progress, the changing forms of production, and class warfare, lies to-day the fact that the old ideals of society have become corrupt, and that this corruption has resulted in dishonesty of life. It is this dishonesty of personal life which is becoming the occasion of a new class-war, from whose fierce parturition-struggle will arise a new ideal—destined to sway human society for many a thousand years, and to give shape to the forms of its industrial, scientific, and artistic life.[1]

The feeling, indeed, seems to be spreading that England stands already on the verge of a dangerous precipice; at any moment the door may open for her on a crisis more serious than any in her whole history. Rotten at heart, and penetrated with falsehood, her aristocracy emasculated of its manhood, her capitalist classes wrapped in selfishness, luxury, and self-satisfied philanthropy, her Government offices—army, navy, and the rest—effete, plethoric, gorged (in snake-like coma) with red tape,[2] her Church sleeping profoundly—snoring aloud—her trading classes steeped in deception and money-greed, her laborers stupefied with overwork and beer, her poorest stupefied with despair, there is not a point which will bear

---

[1] What this new Ideal of Humanity will be I will not attempt here to foreshadow. Sufficient that *honesty*—the honest human relation—must obviously be essential to it. As the ideal of the Feudal Age was upheld and presented to the world in its great poetry, so the new ideal of the Democratic Age will be upheld and presented to the world in the great poetry of Democracy.

[2] An intelligent officer of our own navy, having lately had occasion to inspect one of the naval departments at Washington, tells me that in organisation, alertness, modern information, and despatch of business it altogether surpasses our own corresponding Admiralty department, and leaves it far behind! As to the state of our army departments, we know what that is only too well.

examination, hardly a wheel in the whole machine which will not give way under pressure. The first serious disturbance now, and the wheels will actually cease to go round; the first great strain—European or Eastern war—and it seems not improbable that the governing classes of England will succumb disgracefully. Then—with an exhausting war upon us, our foreign supplies largely cut off, our own country (which might grow ample food for its present population) systematically laid waste and depopulated by landlord legislation, with hopeless commercial depression, stagnation of trade, poverty, and growing furious anarchy—our position will be easier imagined than described.

In the face of such considerations it were well to go straight to the heart of the matter. It were well to consider whether possibly the fate of a great nation may not very profoundly centre round this question of the honesty of its life. The difficulty is that to many people—and to whole classes—mere honesty seems such a small matter. If it were only some great Benevolent Institution to recommend! But this is like Naaman's case in the Bible: to merely bathe in the Jordan and make yourself clean—is really too undignified!

Yet the moment one comes to look into the heart of modern society one perceives how essentially unclean it is—how, after all, the pervading aim and effort of personal life, either consciously or unconsciously entertained, is to maintain ourselves at the cost of others—to live at the expense of other folk's labor, without giving an equivalent of our own labor in return—and if this is not dishonesty I don't know what is!

Let a man pause just for once in the horrid scramble, and ask himself what he really consumes day by day of other people's work—what in the way of food, of clothing, of washing, scrubbing, and the attentions of domestics, or even of his own wife and children—what money he spends in drink, dress, books, pictures, at the theatre, in travel. Let him sternly, and as well as he may, reckon up the sum total by which he has thus made himself indebted to his fellows, and then let him consider what he creates for their benefit in return. Let him strike the balance. Is he a benefactor of society?—is it quits between him and his countrymen and women?—or is he a dependent upon them, a vacuum and a minus quantity?—a beggar, alms-receiver, or thief?

And not only What is he? but What is he trying to be? For on the Ideal hangs the whole question. Here at last we come back to the root of national life. What the ideal cherished by the people at large is, that the nation will soon become. Each individual man is not always sure to realise the state of life that he has in his mind, but in the nation it is soon realised; and if the current idea of individuals is to *get* as much and *give* as little as they can, to be debtors of society and alms-receivers of the labor of others, then you have the spectacle of a nation, as England to-day, rushing on to bankruptcy and ruin, saddled with a huge national debt, and converted into one gigantic workhouse and idle shareholders' asylum. (Imagine a lot of people on an island—all endeavouring to eat other people's dinners, but taking precious care not to provide any of their own—and you will have a picture of what the "well-to-do" on this island succeed in doing, and a lot of people not well-to-do are trying to arrive at.)

For there is no question that this *is* the Ideal of England to-day—to live dependent on others, consuming much and creating next to nothing[1]—to occupy a spacious house, have servants ministering to you, dividends converging from various parts of the world towards you, workmen handing you the best part of their labor as profits, tenants obsequiously bowing as they disgorge their rent, and a good balance at the bank; to be a kind of human sink into which much flows but out of which nothing ever comes—except an occasional putrid whiff of Charity and Patronage—this, is it not the thing which we have before us? which if we have not been fortunate enough to attain to, we are doing our best to reach?

Sad that the words "lady" and "gentleman"— once nought but honorable—should now have become so soiled by all ignoble use. But I fear that nothing can save them. The modern Ideal of Gentility is hopelessly corrupt, and it must be our avowed object to destroy it.

Of course, among its falsities, the point which I am alluding to is the most important. It is absolutely useless for the well-to-do of this country to talk of Charity while they are abstracting the vast sums they do from the laboring classes, or to pretend to alleviate by philanthropic nostrums the frightful poverty

[1] By fine irony called "having an independence."

which they are *creating wholesale by their mode of life.* All the money given by the Church, by charity organisations, by societies or individuals, and all the value of the gratuitous work done by country gentlemen, philanthropists, and others, is a mere drop in the ocean compared with the sums which these same people and their relatives abstract from the poor, under the various legal pretences of interest, dividends, rent, profits, and state-payments of many kinds. "They clean the outside of the cup and platter, but within they are full of *extortion* and *excess.*"

If for every man who consumes more than he creates there must of necessity be another man who has to consume less than he creates, what must be the state of affairs in that nation where a vast class—and ever vaster becoming—is living in the height of unproductive wastefulness? Obviously another vast class—and ever vaster becoming—must be sinking down into the abyss of toil, penury, and degradation. Look at Brighton and Scarborough and Hastings and the huge West End of London, and the polite villa residences which like unwholesome toadstools dot and disfigure the whole of this great land. On *what* are these "noble" mansions of organised idleness built except upon the bent back of poverty and lifelong hopeless unremitting toil! Think! you who live in them, what your life is, and upon what it is founded.

As far as the palaces of the rich stretch through Mayfair and Belgravia and South Kensington, so far (and farther) must the hovels of the poor inevitably stretch in the opposite direction. There is no escape. It is useless to talk about better housing of these unfortunates unless you strike at the root of their poverty; and if you want to see the origin and explanation of an East London rookery, you must open the door and walk in upon some fashionable dinner-party at the West End, where elegance, wealth, ease, good grammar, politeness, and literary and sentimental conversation only serve to cover up and conceal a heartless mockery—the lie that it is a fine thing to live upon the labor of others. You may abolish the rookery, but if you do not abolish the other thing, the poor will only find some other place to die in; and one room in a sanitary and respectable neighborhood will serve a family for that purpose as well as a whole house in a dirtier locality. If this state of affairs were to go on long (which it won't do) England would be converted, as I have said, into one vast workhouse and pauper asylum, in which rows of polite paupers, surrounded by luxuries and daintily fed, would be entirely served and supported by another class—of paupers unable to get bread enough to eat!

But the whole Gentility business is corrupt throughout, and will not bear looking into for a moment. It is incompatible with Christianity (at least as Christ appears to have taught it); it gives a constant lie to the doctrine of human brotherhood.

The wretched man who has got into its toils must surrender that most precious of all things — the human relation to the mass of mankind. He feels a sentimental sympathy certainly for his "poorer brethren"; but he finds that he lives in a house into which it would be simply an insult to ask one of them; he wears clothes in which it is impossible for him to do any work of ordinary usefulness. If he sees an old woman borne down by her burden in the street, he can run to the charity organisation perhaps and get an officer to inquire into her case—but he cannot go straight up to her like a *man*, and take it from her onto his own shoulders; for he is a *gentleman*, and might soil his clothes! It is doubtful even whether—clothes or no clothes, old woman or no old woman—he could face the streets where he is known with a bundle on his shoulders; his dress is a barrier to all human relation with simple people, and his words of sympathy with the poor and suffering are wasted on the wide air while the flash of his jewellery is in their eyes.

He finds himself among people whose constipated manners and frozen speech are a continual denial of all natural affection—and a continual warning against offence; where to say 'onesty is passable, but to say 'ouse causes a positive congestion; where human dignity is at such a low ebb that to have an obvious patch upon your coat would be considered fatal to it; where manners have reached (I think) the very lowest pitch of littleness and *niaiserie;* where human wants and the sacred facts, sexual and other, on which human life is founded, are systematically ignored; where to converse with a domestic at the dinner-table would be an unpardonable breach of etiquette; where it is assumed as a matter of course that you do nothing for yourself—to lighten the burden which your presence in the world necessarily casts upon others; where to be discovered washing

your own linen, or cooking your own dinner, or up to
the elbows in dough on baking day, or helping to get
the coals in, or scrubbing your own floor, or cleaning
out your own privy, would pass a sentence of lifelong
banishment on you; where all dirty work, or at least
such work as is considered dirty by the "educated"
people in a household, is thrust upon young and ignorant girls; where children are brought up to feel
far more shame at any little breach of social decorum
—at an "h" dropped,[1] or a knife used in the wrong
place at dinner, or a wrong appellative given to a
visitor—than at glaring acts of selfishness and un-
charitableness.

In short, the unfortunate man finds himself in a
net of falsehoods; the whole system of life around
him is founded on falsehood. The pure beautiful relation of humanity, the most sacred thing in all this
world, is betrayed at every step; and Christianity

[1] The explanation, as far as I can discover, of this mysterious
iniquity is as follows: It is a notorious tendency in language, as
it progresses, to drop the aspiration. Thus the "h," though
common in Latin, is extinct in the derivative Italian, and only
feebly surviving in French. In English the singular phenomenon presents itself of there being two usages—the "h" being
practically extinct among the mass of the people, while it is
clung to with tenacity by the more or less literary classes (and
with exaggerated tenacity by those who ape these classes). The
explanation seems to be that the natural progress of language
has gone on among the people at large, but has been checked
among the lettered classes by the conservative influence of the
arts of printing and writing. And that it should be possible
for one section of the community thus to slide past the other,
and for two usages so to be established, only illustrates the com
pleteness of class alienation that exists in this country.

with its message of human love, Democracy with its magnificent conception of inward and sacramental human equality, can only be cherished by him in the hidden interior of his being; they can have no real abiding place in his outward life.

And when he turns to the sources from which his living is gained, he only flounders from the quagmire into the bog. The curse of dishonesty is upon him; he can find no bottom anywhere.

The interest of his money comes to him he knows not whence; it is wrung from the labor of someone —he knows not whom. His capital is in the hands of railway companies, and his dividends are gained in due season—but how? He dares not inquire. What have companies, what have directors and secretaries and managers to do with the question whether *justice* is done to the workmen? and when did a shareholder ever rise up and contend that dividends ought to be less and wages more? (There have been one or two cases lately, but they were hissed down.)

His rents come to him from land and houses. Shall he go round and collect them himself? No, that is impossible. This farmer would show him such a desperate balance-sheet, that widow would plead such a piteous tale, this house might be in too disgraceful a state, and entail untold repairs. No, it is impossible. He must employ an agent or steward, and go and live at Paris or Brighton out of sight and hearing of those whose misfortunes might disturb his peace of mind;—or put his money affairs entirely in the hands of a solicitor. *That* is a good way to stifle conscience.

Money entails duties. How shall we get the money and forget the duties? Voilà the great problem! . . . But we cannot forget the duties. They cark unseen.

He has lent out his money on mortgage. Horrid word that "mortgage!"—"foreclosure," too!—sounds like clutching somebody by the throat! Best not go and see the party who is mortgaged;—might be some sad tale come out. Do it through a solicitor, too, and it will be all right.

Thus the unfortunate man of whom I have spoken finds that, turn where he may, the whole of his life — his external life — rests on falsehood. And I would ask you, reader, especially well-to-do and dividend-drawing reader, *is* this —this picture of the ordinary life of English gentility—your Ideal of life? or is it not? For if it is do not be afraid, but please look it straight in the face and understand exactly what it means; but if it is not, then come out of it! It may take you years to *get* out; certainly you will not shake yourself free in a week, or a month, or many months, but still— Come out!

And surely the whole state of society which is founded on this Ideal, however wholesome or fruitful it may have once been, *has* in these latter days (whether we see it or not) become quite decayed and barren and corrupt. It is no good disguising the fact; surely much better is it that it should be exposed and acknowledged. Of those who are involved in this state of society we need think no evil. They are our brothers and sisters, as well as the rest; and oftentimes, consciously or unconsciously, are suffering, caught in its toils.

Why to-day are there thousands and thousands throughout these classes who are weary, depressed, miserable, who discern no object to live for; who keep wondering whether life is worth living, and writing weary dreary articles in magazines on that subject? Who keep wandering from the smoking-room of the club into Piccadilly and the park, and from the park into picture galleries and theatres; who go and "stay" with friends in order to get away from their own surroundings, and seek "change of air," if by any means that may bring with it a change of interest of life? Why, indeed? Except because the human heart (to its eternal glory) cannot subsist on lies; because—whether they know it or not—the deepest truest instincts of their nature are belied, falsified at every turn of their actual lives; and therefore they are miserable, therefore they seek something else, they know not clearly what.

If, looking on England, I have thought that it is time this Thing should come to an end, because of the poverty-stricken despairing multitudes who are yearly sacrificed for the maintenance of it, and (as many a workman has said to me) are put to a *slow death* that it may be kept going, I have at other times thought that, even more for the sake of those who ride in the Juggernaut car itself, to terminate the hydra-headed and manifold misery which lurks deep down behind their decorous exteriors and well-appointed surroundings, should it be finally abolished.

Anyhow, it must go. The hour of its condemnation

has struck. And not only the false thing. I speak to you, working men and women of England, that you should no longer look to the ideal which creates this Thing—that you should no longer look forward to a day when you shall turn your back on your brothers and sisters, and smooth back white and faultless wristbands—living on their labor! but that you shall look to the new Ideal, the ideal of social brotherhood, and of honesty, which, as surely as the sun rises in the morning, shall rise again on our suffering and sorrowing country.

But I think I hear some civilisee say, "Your theories are all very well, and all about honesty and that sort of thing, but it is all quite impracticable. Why, if I were only to consume an equal value to that which I create, I should never get on at all. Let alone cigars and horses and the like, but how about my wife and family? I don't see how I could possibly keep up *appearances*, and if I were to let my position go, all my usefulness (details not given) would go with it. Besides, I really don't see how a man *can* create enough for all his daily wants. Of course, as you say, there must be thousands and millions who are obliged to do so, and *more* (in order to support us), but how the deuce they live I cannot imagine—and they *must* have to work awfully hard. But I suppose it is their business to support us, and I don't see how civilisation would get on without them, and in return, of course, we keep them in order, you know, and give them *lots* of good advice!"

To all which I reply, "Doubtless there is something

very appalling in the prospect of actually maintaining oneself—but I sincerely believe that it is possible. Besides, would not you yourself think it very interesting just to try; if only to see what you would dispense with if you had to do the labor connected with it—or its equivalent? If you had to cook your own dinner, for instance?"

"By Jove! I believe one would do without a lot of sauces and side dishes!"

"Or if you had to do a week's hard work merely to get a new coat—"

"Of course I should make the old one do—only it would become so beastly unfashionable."

That is about it. There are such a lot of things which we could do without—which we really don't want—only, and but . . . . !

And rather than sacrifice these beloved onlies and buts, rather than snip off a few wants, or cut a sorry figure before friends, we rush on with the great crowd which jams and jostles through the gateway of Greed over the bodies of those who have fallen in the struggle. And we enjoy no rest, and our hours of idleness, when they come, are not delightful as they should be. For they are not free and tuneful like the idleness of a ploughboy or a lark, but they are clouded with the spectral undefined remembrance of those at the price of whose blood they have been bought.

As to the difficulty of maintaining oneself, listen to this, please; and read it slowly: "For more than five years I maintained myself thus solely by the labor of my hands; and I found that by working about six weeks in a year I could meet all the expenses of living."

Who was it wrote these extraordinary words?

It has for some time been one of the serious problems of Political Economy to know how much labor is really required to furnish a man with ordinary necessaries. The proportion between labor and its reward has been lost sight of amid the complexities of modern life; and we only know for certain that the ordinary wages of manual labor represent very much less than the value actually created.

Fortunately for us, however, about forty years ago a man thoroughly tired of wading through the bogs of modern social life had the pluck to land himself on the dry ground of actual necessity. He squatted on a small piece of land in New England, built himself a little hut, produced the main articles of his own food, hired himself out now and then for a little ready money, and has recorded for us, as above, the results of his experience. Moreover, to leave no doubt as to his meaning, he adds, "The whole of my winters, as well as most of my summers, I had free and clear for study." (He was an author and naturalist.)

The name of this man was Henry Thoreau. His book "Walden"—and anyone can obtain it now [1]— gives the details of the experiment by which he proved that a man can actually maintain himself, and have abundant leisure besides! And this, too, under circumstances of considerable disadvantage; for Thoreau isolated himself to a great extent from the

[1] Camelot Classics: W. Scott, London. 1886. Price 1s.

co-operation of his fellows, and had to contend single-handed with Nature in the midst of the woods, where his crops were sadly at the mercy of wild creatures. It is true, as I have said, that he had built himself a hut, and had two or three acres of land to start with; but what a margin does his six weeks in a year leave for critical subtractions!

If anyone, however, doubts the truth of the general statement contained in the last paragraph—*i.e.*, that a man can maintain himself and have abundant leisure besides—his doubt must surely be removed by a study of the conditions of life in England in the fifteenth century. At that time, between the fall of the feudal barons and the rise of the capitalists and the modern landlords, there was an interval during which the workers actually got something like their due, and were not robbed to a very great extent by the classes above them. Thorold Rogers, in his "Work and Wages," gives the wages of an *unskilled* town-laborer at 6d. a day in the fifteenth century, while the price of a sheep at that time was 2s. *Now* the proportions are 3s. to 50s. Four centuries ago the laborer could have bought the sheep with four days' work; *now* he requires the toil of sixteen or seventeen days. Similarly with the price of an ox, which was then 20s. Even bread he could earn with less work then than now. Why is this? Surely our country is not at present so overgrazed and cultivated as to increase the difficulty of raising beasts and crops (on the contrary, it is half-deserted and *under*-cultivated); nor, certainly, did the laborer in the fifteenth century receive *more* than he might be said to have created by his labor. Why, then, does the laborer to-day not get anything like that reward? The reason is obvious. His labor is as fruitful as ever, but the greater part of its produce—its reward—is taken from him.

As fruitful as ever?—far more fruitful than ever; for we have taken no account of the vast evolutions of machinery. What that reward would be, under our greatly-increased powers of production—if it were only righteously distributed—we may leave to be imagined.

As to Thoreau, the real truth about him is that he was a thorough economist. He reduced life to its simplest terms, and having, so to speak, labor in his right hand and its reward in his left, he had no difficulty in seeing what was worth laboring for and what was not, and no hesitation in discarding things that he did not think *worth* the time or trouble of production.

And I believe myself that the reason why he could so easily bring himself to do without these things, and thus became free—"presented with the freedom," of nature and of life—was that he was a thoroughly educated man in the true sense of the word.

It seems to be an accepted idea nowadays that the better educated anyone is the more he must require. "A ploughman can do on so much a year, but an educated man—O quite impossible!"

Allow me to say that I regard this idea as entirely false. First of all, if it *were* true, what a dismal prospect it would open out to us! The more educated we became the more we should require for our support, the worse bondage we should be in to material things. We should have to work continually harder and harder to keep pace with our wants, or else to trench more and more on the labor of others; at each step the more complicated would the problem of existence become.

But it is entirely untrue. Education, if decently conducted, does not turn a man into a creature of blind wants, a prey to ever fresh thirsts and desires— it brings him *into relation with the world around him*. It enables a man to derive pleasure and to draw sustenance from a thousand common things, which bring neither joy nor nourishment to his more enclosed and imprisoned brother. The one can beguile an hour anywhere. In the field, in the street, in the workshop, he sees a thousand things of interest. The other is bored, he must have a toy—a glass of beer or a box at the opera.

Besides, the educated man, if truly educated, has surely more resources of skilful labor to fall back upon—he need not fear about the future. The other may do well to accumulate a little fund against a rainy day.

It is only to education commonly so-called—the false education—that these libels apply. I admit that to the current education of the well-to-do they do apply, but *that* is only or mainly a cheap-jack education, an education in glib phrases, grammar, and the art of keeping up appearances, and has little to do with bringing anyone into relation with the real world around him—the real world of Humanity, of honest daily Life, of the majesty of Nature, and the wonderful questions and answers of the soul, which out of these are whispered on everyone who fairly faces them.

Let us then have courage. There is an ideal before us, which is attainable, not very difficult of attainment, and which true education will help us to attain to, not lead us astray from.

A man may, if he likes, try the experiment of Thoreau, and restrict himself to the merest necessaries of life—so as to see how much labor it really requires to live.[1] Starting from that zero point, he may add to his luxuries and to his labors as he thinks fit. How far he travels along that double line will of course depend upon temperament. Thoreau, as I have said, made a speciality of economy. One day he picked up a curiosity and kept it on his shelf for a time; but soon finding that it required dusting he threw it out of the window! It did not pay for its keep. Thoreau preferred leisure to ornaments; other people may prefer ornaments to leisure. There is of course no prejudice—all characters, temperaments, and idiosyncracies are welcome and thrice welcome. The only condition is that you must not expect to have the ornaments and the idleness both. If you choose to live in a room full of ornaments, no one can make the slightest possible objection; but you must not expect society (in the form of your maidservant) to dust them for you, unless you do something useful for

[1] It must be remembered, however, that if anyone under present conditions of society tried this experiment as a wage-laborer, he would be badly handicapped, as he would not receive anything like the reward of his labor.

society in return. (I need not at this time of day say that giving Money is not equivalent to "doing something useful"—unless you have fairly earned the money; then it is.)

Let us have courage. There is ample room within this ideal of Honest Life for all human talent, ingenuity, divergency of thought and temperament. It is not a narrow cramped ideal. How can it be ?—for it *alone* contains in it the possibility of human brotherhood. But I warn you: it is *not* compatible with that other ideal of Worldly Gentility. I do not say this lightly. I know what it is for anyone to have to abandon the forms in which he has been brought up; nor do I wish to throw discredit on any one class, for I know that this ideal permeates more or less the greater part of the nation to-day. But the hour demands fidelity. There is no time now for temporising. England stands on the brink of a crisis in which no wealth, no armaments, no diplomacy will save her—only an awakening of the National Conscience. If this comes she will live—if it comes not * * * ?

The canker of effete gentility has eaten into the heart of this nation. Its noble men and women are turned into toy ladies and gentlemen; the eternal dignity of (voluntary) Poverty and Simplicity has been forgotten in an unworthy scramble for easychairs. Justice and Honesty have got themselves melted away into a miowling and watery philanthropy; the rule of honor between master and servant, and servant and master, between debtor and creditor, and buyer and seller, has been turned into a rule of dishonor, concealment, insincere patronage, and sharp bargains; and England lies done to death by her children who should have loved her.

As for you, working-men and working-women—in whom now, if anywhere, the hope of England lies—I appeal to you at any rate to cease from this ideal, I appeal to you to cease your part in this gentility business — to cease respecting people because they wear fine clothes and ornaments, and because they live in grand houses. You know you do these things, or pretend to do them, and to do either is foolish. We have had ducking and forelock-pulling enough It is time for *you* to assert the dignity of human labor. I do not object to a man saying "sir" to his equal, or to an elder, but I do object to his saying "sir" to broadcloth or to a balance at the bank. Why don't you say "yes" and have done with it? Remember that you, too, have to learn the lesson of honesty. You know that in your heart of hearts you despise this nonsense; you know that when the "gentleman's" back is turned you take off his fancy airs, and mimic his incapable importances, or launch out into bitter abuse of one who you think has wronged you. Would it not be worthier, if you have these differences, not to conceal them, but for the sake of your own self-respect to face them out firmly and candidly?

The re-birth of England cannot come without sacrifices from you, too. On the contrary, whatever is done, you will have to do the greater part of it. You will often have to incur the charge of disrespect; you will have to risk, and to lose, situations; you will have to bear ridicule, and, perhaps, arms; Anarchists, Socialists, Communists you will hear yourselves called. But what would you have? It is no good preaching Democracy with your mouths, if you are going to stand all the while and prop with your shoulders the rotten timbers of Feudalism—of which, riddled as they have been during three centuries by the maggots of Usury, we need say no worse than that it is time they should fall.

I say from this day you must set to work yourselves in word, thought, and deed, to root out this genteel dummy—this hairdresser's Ideal of Humanity—and to establish yourselves (where you stand) upon the broad and sacred ground of human labor. As long as you continue to send men to Parliament because they ride in carriages, or cannot have a meeting without asking a "squire," whom you secretly make fun of, to take the chair, or must have clergymen and baronets patrons of your benefit clubs—so long are you false to your natural instincts, and to your own great destinies.

Be arrogant rather than humble, rash rather than stupidly contented; but, best of all, be firm, helpful towards each other, forgetful of differences, scrupulously honest in yourselves, and charitable even to your enemies, but determined that *nothing* shall move you from the purpose you have set before you—the righteous distribution in society of the fruits of your own and other men's labor, the return to Honesty as the sole possible basis of national life and national safety, and the redemption of England from the curse which rests upon her.

MODERN MONEY-LENDING,

AND THE

MEANING OF DIVIDENDS.

"If I lend £100, and for it covenant to receive £105, or any other sum greater than was the sum I did lend, this is that that we call usury; such a kind of bargaining as no good man, or godly man, ever used."—*Bp. Jewell.*

"Chi fila ha una camiccia, e chi non fila ne ha due."

THE practice of Money-lending is now carried out on such an enormous scale, and by such a large class of society, and is attended by certain evils so widespread and disastrous, that it has become fairly necessary to look the problem in the face; and whatever may be the conclusion arrived at, I shall consider the purpose of this paper fulfilled if it causes the reader (and myself) to confront the question, and to see that it requires solution.

There has always been a disagreeable odor about this trade. The very word Usury has unpleasant associations with it. How is it then that we who reprobate the money-lending Jew of mediæval Europe and the marwari whose loans press so heavily to-day upon the peasant of India, are light-hearted enough to lend our money out at interest without a qualm, and (some of us) to make our entire subsistence on the gains so got from other people ?

Is it that the Shylock and the marwari are so distant from us that we do not perceive our relationship to them ?

"No," says someone, "the reason is that they practised and practise Usury; we only reap Interest. To live on the gains of other people becomes criminal when you depass a certain point."

What then is that point ? Where is that line to be drawn which divides legitimate Interest from Usury ? Let us remember that the word Usury simply indicates that the person who lends the money expects a reward for the use of it; and the word Interest indicates that the person who lends the money is interested in, or a party to, the concern from which the gain is expected to be made. There is nothing in the original signification of the two words to show one proceeding as more legitimate than the other.

Certainly it is quite conceivable that a high rate of Interest might be grossly unfair, and a low rate only just and equitable; but this distinction of degree can hardly be the ground of *our* action, since there is nothing that we usually covet more or congratulate ourselves more upon than the obtaining of a high rate of interest for our money.

No—the reason, it seems to me, why we carry on our money-lending business without qualms lies simply in the fact that the practice, in its modern form, is universal round us. Every body (which in the "society" signification of the word means everyone who does not work with his hands) does it. Custom sanctions it; "the law allows it." And to most people involved in the practice it naturally never occurs to consider its rightfulness or wrongfulness at all.

But this does not make it the less incumbent on us—once we have looked into the matter—to get to the roots of it. Rather more. Let us dig into it then.

The fundamental principle of social life and just living can never, it seems to me, be too often brought forward. For some reason or other it is only too often liable to be obscured. It is this—that the existence and well-being of a people are secured by their collective labor, and that only by taking his part in that labor can each man have a right to the advantages which flow from it. Political Economy always begins with an island! At first all are workers, and by a few hours' work daily from each man sufficient of the necessaries and adornments even of life are produced (from the natural resources of the island) to maintain every one in comfort. After a time it is found that the state of affairs has changed. Half the population is now living in idleness—or at most engaged in occupations whose benefit to the community is very remote and dubious. The other half is working very hard—twice as many hours a day, in fact, as before—as it must do to keep things up to the former level.

This is a sad change for the worse. One half of the community is living in degrading slavery, has more work to do than can be done without injury and the blunting of noble powers. The other half is living in (even more) degrading dependence, and is suffering that injury to its soul which comes and must come from all meanness and selfishness.

This second state of affairs on the island is what we notice on our own island to-day and in modern social life at large. The causes which have led up to it and the means by which it is kept going are manifold. The use of money and of capital, hereditary acquirements, monopoly of land, customs and laws now grown false and harmful, are some of the engines by which one part of the community retains its power over the other part. The problem of the little island is complicated, too, when we come to consider the big island, by such matters as foreign trade, taxes, misunderstandings as to the nature of money, and all the cog-wheels big and little of social life—*but* essentially it is the same. These things only serve to disguise the fact that one class is living on the labor of another; they do not in any way alter the fact.

Let us look at the matter again. I have said that the money-lending classes are in our modern society very large. They are also greatly on the increase. It can hardly be otherwise. Let us suppose that in some society conducted on our present system *one* man (and only one at first) accumulates enough money to bring him in a substantial income—say £500 a year. Then that man is safe. He has escaped from the labor of feeding himself and children, and may fold his arms and amuse himself as he likes—he has got on the dry land beyond the flood—and this in perpetuity practically; for he may live as long as he can and then transmit the right to those who come

THE MEANING OF DIVIDENDS. 27

after him. He is safe, and except by his own imprudence need never again join the throng of those who toil and spin. Presently another man accumulates the desired amount. He also "retires," and is safe. Then a third and fourth. Then hundreds and thousands, then a considerable portion of the whole nation—where shall we stop? All the footsteps (with but few exceptions) point the same way. Few, who by their own exertions or those of their fathers and grandfathers have reached the desired haven, are likely to quit it again. The number *must* go on increasing—yet it is impossible for a whole nation to retire and suck its thumb! What is happening? This is happening—a vast and ever vaster proportion of the nation is getting (by force of existing social rights and machinery) to live on the labor of the rest. Every day, of those who are harnessed to the car of national life and prosperity, one or another by dint of extra forethought, prudence, miserliness, cunning, or whatever it may be, gets an advantage over the rest, leaves them, jumps *inside* the car, and thenceforth instead of drawing is drawn. The end is only too obvious. It is a *reductio ad absurdum* of national life. It is breakdown, smash up—and the car left in the ditch.

These are serious charges to bring against the practice of money-lending as carried on in modern society. Let us look at the other side of the question.

I have £500 which I have saved out of the products of my own labor—and which I have no immediate use for. My neighbor offers me 5 per cent. per annum for the use of the sum for a given period.

Have I not a perfect right to accept his offer? Should I not be a perfect fool if I refused it?

Yes (in answer to the first question—the answer to the second will, perhaps, appear later on) I have a perfect (legal) right to accept his offer. On this view Interest is a gratuity. It is presumably a payment made by the borrower in return for some advantage he derives from the money lent. It does not matter to me in a sense how he employs the money. He may merely squander it for his own amusement, or he may employ it as capital to bring him a profit. In either case he gives me what I consider sufficient security for its repayment, and if he offers me 5 per cent. interest besides it is because the advantage is worth that to him; and I have a perfect right to accept it.

Besides, am I not by lending this money actually in the second case benefiting society? Do I not put capital into the hands of a man who is willing and able to employ it, and thus actually encourage and further production? Nay more, I may go further, and waiving my request for a security may subscribe my funds directly to his concern, taking the risk and sharing some of the profits—may become a shareholder, in fact. In doing this do I not benefit my country, and may I not pocket my returns with a glow of substantial and generous satisfaction?[1]

---

[1] Under the term Money-lenders, I thus include both Bond and Shareholders—receivers of Interest and sharers of Profits. I am aware that current Political Economy draws a considerable distinction between these two classes. But though for scientific purposes such a distinction may be useful, yet practi-

Yes, I believe that it is possible that in the ways mentioned I *may* be useful to society; and it seems to me possible that, for instance, the Jew money-lender of the thirteenth and fourteenth centuries in England *was* a useful member of society. At that time, when capital was scarce, and for the budding demands of commerce private individuals could often not supply sufficient funds, his services may have been indispensable; and if he sometimes took undue advantage of his position, plentiful laws restrained him.

How then can it be that the gains of the modern money-lender, whether bond or shareholder, should lead to such disastrous conclusions as I have pointed out? How can we reconcile the supposed rightfulness of interest with the immorality of a life of idleness, and the meanness of a vast class supported by the excessive and exhausting labor of the mass of the people?

Is it possible that a practice which may be wholesome and useful to society in a moderate or small degree and at one period, may become highly dangerous when carried out on a large scale and at another period; that the Jew money-lender, in consideration of his services, could in his time really be tolerated, but that the shareholder has become an insupportable Old Man of the Sea, who must be torn off and got rid of at all costs? Quite possible, I think; though I will not by any means say that this brings us to the bottom of the whole matter. Let us dig at it again.

Is it still not obvious that the poverty of the mass

cally, and as far as regards national advantage or social morality, I confess I do not see that it is of much importance.

of the people stands in direct relationship to the wealth of the money-lending classes, that they are the two opposite sides or faces, in fact, of the same thing? Has that original illustration about the people on the island grown dim by reason of some considerations by the way which have been introduced? Let it stand out clear again. It cannot be got over.

Where does Interest come from? Have you ever thought of that?

If I lend £500 to a man, he may, as I have said, either squander it away or invest it as capital to bring him in a profit. The first case need not detain us long; it is in the main an exceptional case. If the borrower squanders my money, I shall probably have to sell him up to repay myself capital and interest; I shall not lend to him again, and that game soon comes to an end. The money-lending which constitutes the great problem of modern society, is that which is connected in some way or other with capital. I lend my £500 to a man who employs it as capital in some concern, and the interest which I receive comes out of the profits of that concern.

But where does it come from? Who pays it? How does the capitalist make his profit?

The capitalist buys raw material; he employs labor to work it up into a finished article; and he sells the finished article. These are the three processes of his business, and in one (or more) of these processes he must get more than he gives—otherwise he can make no profit. That is quite clear, I think. He is a clothier. He buys cloth, employs men and

THE MEANING OF DIVIDENDS. 31

women to cut and stitch it, and sells coats. The coat contains so much cloth and so much added labor (including the labor necessary to replace the wear and tear of the sewing machines). And the value of the coat is equal to the value of the cloth plus the value of the labor put into it.

It is obvious that in the long run the coat will not sell for more than this. But if not, where does his profit come from? It must come out of the cloth or out of the labor. But he has paid the full value of the cloth in purchasing it, and, therefore, he cannot, on the average, get more in selling it. Has he paid the full value of the labor in purchasing *that?* No, certainly not; and it is not difficult to see that it is here that his profit arises. He gives his young women eighteenpence (generally less) for their day's work at the sewing machines. But the labor they put into the cloth is *worth* far more than eighteenpence; and the value that he gets in the market for the coat (above the value of the cloth out of which it is made) is the actual value of the labor put into it, not the value of the wretched wage which he gives. Thus it is that he gets more than he gives.

The process is simple enough. An article for whose entire production the total sum of labor expended is nine hours will fetch on the average in the market an equivalent of nine hours' labor, *e.g.*, such an amount of coin as would on the average cost nine hours' labor in its production. So if the workwoman puts nine hours' labor into the coat, she will at any rate increase the value of the coat on the market by that equivalent sum. But does anyone for a moment suppose that the eighteenpence which she receives is the equivalent, or anything like the equivalent, of those same nine hours?[1] What, if you please, in the way of the ordinary necessaries of life does nine hours' labor represent? Godwin, the author of "Political Justice," calculated that a man with ordinary labor, unhampered by the rapacity of others, should be able in two hours daily to supply himself with the necessaries and conveniences of life. Bastiat, if I am not mistaken, mentions two and a half hours. Karl Marx, whose calculations on capital I am following, supposes six hours' labor per diem necessary, in order that a man may provide for himself, a wife, and two children. Of course an exact estimate on this subject is difficult to make. So far has society got from any simple and equitable relation between labor and its reward that we actually *do not know* how much (or how little) labor is required for a man to support himself in health and comfort (see p. 12). But all authors agree that it is very small compared with the nine hours' daily slavery which constitute the beginning and the end of a modern working man's life.

The nine hours' labor, then, which our sempstress or machinist puts into the article *ought* to represent for her a comfortable subsistence for several days. It represents a bare living for one day. She ought to get, say, a value of 6s. for it. She receives 1s. 6d. The capitalist pockets the difference. The wretched girl makes him a present, or *has* to make him a pre-

[1] Twelve hours, with one and a half off for meals, is the more usual day's work, I believe, in this department.

sent, of four days' work in the week. She gets the value of her labor for two. And this is where profits, where interest, under our present social system, come from.

The position of women in these matters is notoriously bad, but that of the male laborers, skilled or unskilled, is little better. Marx calculates that the ordinary cotton-spinner makes a present to his master of three days' work in the week. He puts six days' labor into the yarn, and his master in selling the cotton gets the equivalent of that six days' labor, but he only gives the spinner the money value of three days' labor. "Under the old system of *corvée* a man was obliged to give, say one day's work in the week, or at most two, to his feudal lord without any payment. Such a man, though he had the remaining five or six days wholly to himself, was thought little better than a slave. Nor was he. English capitalists would, of all men, subscribe largely to relieve human beings from continuing in such a shameful and degraded position. But here at home, we have men, women, and children, who are obliged to give four, five, six hours a day to the capitalist for nothing, and yet are thought free."[1]

Now let us take the case of a railway company (I am interested in this as I am a shareholder myself, and should like to see how my dividends arise).

We (the shareholders) have subscribed the funds, and—to simplify the matter—we will suppose that we have bought over with a large portion of them the

[1] "England for All," by H. M. Hyndman, price 6d.—An excellent little book.

entire plant of an old company. This then forms our capital stock; and we can begin running trains at once. We shall have to maintain the permanent way and the rolling stock, and for this purpose shall have to employ a large number of men, besides purchasing materials from time to time; and we shall have a large staff of general servants and officials. Our chief expenditure, therefore, will be in wages. And our receipts will arise principally from the transport of goods and passengers. How do we expect to make our profits? Obviously by reducing the expenditure below the receipts.

We have to transport 20 truck-loads of coal. There is a lot of labor required. There is the labor of shunters and signalmen, of station-masters and plate-layers, of driver, stoker, and guard; there is the labor of those who replace the wear and tear of the line and of the rolling stock. All this labor and much more has to be considered. When totted up it constitutes the labor-value of the service rendered. What we expect to get in exchange for the service is an equivalent labor-value as expressed in money—that is to say, if we get £5 for the service it may be supposed that the labor necessary for the production of a piece of gold, value £5, is equivalent to the labor involved in the transport of the said 20 truck-loads of coal. This is the basis of all just exchange. It is possible, however, that we may get more than our labor-value. If we are secure from competition or have a monopoly of any kind, we may succeed in getting more than we give—simply because our customers cannot get their transport done at a less price

THE MEANING OF DIVIDENDS. 35

through other channels. It is possible also that we may sometimes have to take actually less than the labor-value of our services rendered. How we can do this and yet make a profit we shall see presently.

The obvious method, through all this, of securing dividends, is to *keep down wages*.

Let us take the three cases supposed. Let us first assume that the price we can get for our service represents exactly the just exchange—that we receive a labor-value from our customer exactly equal to that which we give him. How do we make our profits? How must we make our profits? Obviously by giving our own servants and workmen *less* than the labor-value of what they do for us—by giving them wages which do *not* represent their labor—which are not an equivalent for it.

Let us suppose, secondly, that competition with another company forces us for the time being to accept from the customer actually less than the labor-value of the service rendered; then obviously we are driven to lower still further the wages of our servants, to do them a more glaring injustice—that is, if we can; for on this depend our chances of a dividend.

These two cases are, I take it, by far the most common. Lately, for instance, large bodies of signalmen working on the Midland Railway have had their wages reduced from 21s. to 19s. a week! These men are working 12 hours a day; one week, nights; another week, days; and some hours on Sundays—some 80 hours in all. Hardly threepence an hour. It is impossible to pretend that these men are paid for their work, but it is the balance of their unpaid labor which creates what is called the dividend; and that is what makes the directors so anxious to reduce the wage.[1]

I can buy in the street six boxes of matches for a penny. The capitalist must sell them at considerably less than that—say nine boxes for a penny. It is difficult for me to believe that the labor-value involved in the making of nine boxes of matches is not more than a penny. If so, this is a case in which the capitalist gets actually less value from the customer than he gives. What then must he give to his own workpeople? Well, we know well enough; we know the shameful wages, 6s. and 7s. a week, which the work-girls receive in this most unhealthy of trades. And this is what the cheapness of matches means.

To return to my railway. The third case remains unconsidered, in which I succeed in getting from my customer (for one reason or another, generally monopoly) *more* than the value of the service rendered. When this happens I certainly *can* pay my servants and workmen the full value of their labor, and yet have a margin for my own profit. And it

[1] Their consideration for the workers may be judged by the following:—Lately the Midland Railway receipts (owing to bad trade) fell off by £50,000 in one half-year. If this had been economised out of dividend, the dividend for the half-year would have been decreased by *one-twentieth part*. But rather than that the shareholders should bear so trifling a loss, it was resolved to recoup the sum out of wages; and this involved the discharge of some *hundreds* of servants, and the reduction of the wages of others in the shameful manner shown above. And yet the Midland Railway is worked as liberally as any railway in the United Kingdom. See note, p. 37.

THE MEANING OF DIVIDENDS. 37

would be useless to deny that this sometimes takes place. Workmen under the present system and with existing fluctuations in trade *sometimes* get in wages as much as represents the full value of their labor. But this is always an exceptional condition of affairs, and does not last long. In such a case where do the profits of capital come from? If I charge my passenger for transporting him from Dover to London the full value of one man's labor for a day, and the human labor actually involved in the transport (reckoning up everything) has been only equal to one man's labor for three-quarters of a day—and I pay my servants justly for that—then I gain my profits clearly out of the passenger. I gain a quarter-day's labor from him—that is, I cause him (or if he does not work himself, whoever works for him) to work a whole day for a service which only costs me (or my representatives) the labor of three-quarters of a day.

Thus, once more, it appears that my profits come, and must come, from the labor of others. They arise, and can only arise, from the fact that some portion of the labor connected with my business goes unremunerated. The proper remuneration of that portion I pocket for myself, and that is how my dividends arise.[1]

---

[1] Any railway company's report will illustrate these remarks. I quote the following figures from the accounts of the North-Eastern for the latter part of 1884. The total revenue for that half-year was £3,299,000. This enormous sum was expended as follows:—Wages (including salaries of officials), £1,078,000; purchase of materials, law costs, taxes, etc., £689,000; and the balance, £1,531,000, went almost entirely to the bond and share holders! That is, roughly speaking, one million sterling went

That labor is the underlying basis of exchangeable value is now assumed, I believe, by most Political Economists; that it is the source of all that is generally termed "Wealth" is obvious. It therefore needs no detailed argument to prove that if a class lives without labor, if it obtains wealth without working for it—it must be appropriating the labor of others, and the wealth that rightfully belongs to them. And this is the case, I fear, of the shareholder and of that vast class in this nation who live on interest and dividends.

But, it may well be asked, if this appropriation is unjust, why does the worker submit to it? Why does he allow a portion, and often a large portion, of his daily labor to go unremunerated?

The answer is: Because he cannot help himself. He sees and feels that it is unjust, but he is caught in the jaws of a vice and cannot move.

The matter lies in a nutshell. If the worker could employ himself, be his own capitalist, then (and then only) could he get the full remuneration of his labor, for he would have no idle person to support in addition to himself and family. But in the existing state of affairs he cannot become his own capitalist. Why? Because, of the two outlets of capital—agriculture and

to the workers who carried on the line, and one million and a half to the idlers who claimed interest on their capital; or, in other words, out of every ten hours that the signalman, engine-driver, or other servant or official worked, he gave six hours for the benefit of the share and bond holder, and only had four for himself. And this is about an average case. Taking the railways of the United Kingdom as a whole, we find that £33,000,000 a year is paid as interest on capital out of this industry alone!

THE MEANING OF DIVIDENDS.

Industrial production—one is barred by our land system, the other by machinery.

In fact, if our workman, having saved up a little capital, proposes to buy a small piece of land and support himself upon it by his own labor, and that of his family—he finds himself at the very outset met by the fact that he can hardly find such a piece of land to buy. The main portion of Great Britain is in the hands of a few thousand large owners. The quantity of land in the market is small, it is mostly in large and cumbrous holdings, the price is prohibitive, and the legal expenses and complications attending the transfer are very vexatious and costly; the result being that in his own country the workman finds himself an exile, without a foot of soil which he can call his own, and unable to exert the force which he longs to put into the ground, without hiring himself out, becoming a slave, a dependent, and giving half the profits of his toil to someone else.

If, on the other hand, he desires to embark his small savings in some form of industrial production, and to employ himself in that way, he finds that machinery forbids. For without machinery he cannot hope to compete in the market. And to acquire machinery and all that goes with it, he must lay out large sums of money, and be a large capitalist at once.

Thus, absolutely unable on the present system to employ himself, the workman is thrown on the market—there to *sell his labor* to the capitalist for what he can get.

Now we begin to perceive the operation of those

two deities, worshipped by Commercial Philosophers
—Supply and Demand. Think for a moment of the
vast floating, fluctuating, tramping, toiling population
that does the manual work of England to-day. "In
the fifteenth century a landless, houseless family was
almost unknown." What material for reflection lies
in these words! Think of the vast patient toiling
population of to-day, homeless, tramping from place
to place, thrice blessed when it can get into some
squalid corner of workshop or factory and *be allowed*
to grind at one eternal and monotonous operation for
nine hours a day; remember that this population is
so situated that it cannot employ itself; and then
think of the capitalist class rolling through the streets
in its carriages, monopolising the land and the instruments of production—at whose feet this working
population has to kneel and beg for employment. Is
it not a mockery to talk of Supply and Demand—or
if not a mockery, are these two words so to rule us
that all charity and human pity, nay, that mere
honesty and the demands of simple justice are to be
set aside in their favor? The Demand is a demand
for bread, the Supply—well, what is the supply?
What is it as a matter of fact, what is it likely to be,
from a class in power to a class that is forced to come
and crouch at its feet? What has it been all the
world over, from the tyrant to the slave? A supply,
alas! of insults and mockery, of kicks supplemented
by patronage and good advice.

The supply (in wages) is and obviously must be
under the present system just sufficient to keep the
laborer going—and, in the long run, no more. I

THE MEANING OF DIVIDENDS. 41

think practically all Political Economists admit this. That whatever fluctuations there may be owing to the state of trade, whatever great accessions in the production of wealth owing to new and ever new mechanical inventions, in the end the wages of the workmen do tend, and must under the capitalist system tend, ever downwards to that minimum which just admits of the support of the workman, and the perpetuation of his race. Capital, in fact, is limited in the hands of the few, and Labor is at the mercy of these few as to whether it shall be employed or not. The country may be full of Labor desiring to be employed, but if the capitalists do not see a way of turning it to their profit, it remains unemployed. The object of all production, in fact, is not the providing for the people or the supply of the wants of the nation—but the profit of a small class. And if the small class is not profited the nation may starve ! That is the long and short of it.

Nothing can illustrate this more decisively than England at the present time. The land holds thousands of men, honest, excellent workmen, who hate idleness and desire work. Can anyone doubt that England would be a richer, happier country if they were employed ? If those men were only turned out on the farm-lands now in every county running to thistles and docks—there to support *themselves* by their own labor—the country would by that alone be millions of pounds richer. Yet these men roam the roads and with hungry eyes look over the hedges at fields all going to waste, at badly-drained, uncared-for, half-cultivated lands—in vain—because, forsooth !

the capitalist and the landlord do not find it suit their pockets to employ them, or even to let them work. The same remark applies to industrial production. It is useless to say that there is not ample work for the industrial classes of England to do—work which would and must be profitable to themselves and the nation. The real question is whether it suits the employing classes to let them do it. But Lord Broadacre and Mr. Moneybag find they can get 10 per cent. for their money in Mexican and Brazilian bonds, and it suits them very well to let their capital go out of the country—suits *them* better perhaps than employing the starving laborers in it. It matters not to them—it matters not to the great shareholding, dividend-drawing, and rent-receiving classes of this country what the condition is of the laboring masses from whom they draw their wealth, so long as they are only able to draw it without being called upon to toil for it themselves.

And it is very curious to see how this fact—this fact that the wage-worker is mulcted of the fruits of his toil, and only receives in wages a fraction of the value he produces—lies at the root, and is the main cause, of all the evils of gluts, commercial depressions and trade-paralysis, which have so puzzled the scientific and so tormented the practical world. I do not say there may not be collateral influences at work; but a little attention will, I think, show that the following is the chief cause. Since the wage-workers, the mass of the people—say of the United Kingdom —receive in wages only a portion (say a half—and this will on the average not be far from the mark) of

THE MEANING OF DIVIDENDS. 43

the value which they actually produce and distribute, it is evident that in any given time, say a year, they will only be able to buy back *one-half* of the goods they have thus put on the market during that time. Who then buys the other half of the goods? Clearly not the capitalist and landlord classes. They—though they receive the money-credits sufficient to enable them to buy the other half—do not really buy to this amount; for being few in number, they cannot possibly use this enormous mass of goods; besides, we know as a matter of fact that they save up a large part of their money-credits and reinvest them abroad.[1]

Hence at the end of a year there remains a mass of goods, a considerable fraction of the total produced during the year, which is not bought either by the masses or the classes—by the masses because they have not the money, by the classes because they do not want the goods.

What becomes of this balance? It remains over to the next year. But the next year the same thing happens over again; and so at the end of that year there is a large balance and accumulation of unbought stuff. By the third or fourth year it is evident that the output will have to be reduced by the diminution of the number of wage-workers, and the discharge of men from employment; but this in its turn reduces

---

[1] Of course if this reinvestment took place at home it would mean the purchase of some of the unbought goods (machinery, etc.); but it is obvious that, as the market at home is from the nature of the case already overstocked, very little such reinvestment takes place here, but the money-credits are sent to new countries.

the buying power of the masses (though not to the same degree), and so several years of stagnant trade have to elapse before Demand catches up the reduced Supply and things right themselves at all. When this happens trade becomes brisk again, and the engine makes another start—but only of course to block itself again in a few years; and so it goes on. If any engineer were to make a machine on such a principle he would be disgraced for life.

But now supposing the wage-worker received in wages the full value of his product (with only the very small deduction necessary for the outlay of capital towards the future, which outlay would then take place at home), then clearly the whole mass of goods produced in a year would be bought up during the same time, and nothing of the nature of a *general* glut or trade depression could possibly ensue. As long as any goods were needed by any section of the population it would *pay* the nation to produce those goods; for that section of the population, being set in employment to produce the goods, would receive in wages sufficient to enable it to buy back the goods it had produced; and the markets would always be lively, and the people always well clothed and shod. But then there could be no individual appropriation of profits and rents by shareholders and landlords, only that due saving by the nation which would be necessary for the continuance of its business towards the future. Thus we see that it is this profit-greed of the present day which lies at the root of bad trade, and which inevitably in the end, like all idiotic things, must stultify and destroy itself.

THE MEANING OF DIVIDENDS. 45

Let me here pause to resume. In considering the morality of Interest I agreed that if one should offer me 5 per cent. interest for the use of my £500 I should have a perfect right to accept it. How far do I feel my conclusion now modified by the foregoing investigations? A perfect *legal* right. Yes, that under the present conditions of society I certainly have. But what sort of right beyond that? what sort of human or moral right?

I confess that if the laborer from whose overplus of work my interest comes were himself in a substantial and flourishing condition, if for instance as in the fifteen century he were himself a small landholder, and employer of his own right arm, then, though I might have compunctions, I should still feel that he had a choice in the matter—that he was really at liberty to bargain with me on equal terms, and to pay me the overplus of his labor or withhold it as he might think fit. But as the circumstances are—seeing that the laborer has no choice, that I practically have him by the throat, and that he must either pay me or die, I fear it is a little out of place to talk of any kind of right at all—except that which comes of force.

Think once more of our island. There are two parties on it. One party possesses all the land (best not inquire how it got it!) and all the tools and implements of industry; the other party possesses nothing. The second party has to do all the labor. Of the fruits of its labor just enough is awarded to it to keep it alive and fit for work, the rest is claimed by the first party (under the names of rent, interest, profit, etc.) as a reward for its kindness in allowing the laborers to use its land and tools!

Why does the second party submit to anything so absurd? Simply because it is the most patient, broad-backed, good-humored, simple creature imaginable, and has never fairly opened its eyes to see through the juggle imposed upon it. But that flam cannot last long now. The day of the rule of class-greed and wealth is almost at an end. The workers are waking up in England and all over Europe to their true position. In a few, very few, years the antagonism will be declared on both sides. Perhaps in England the very next great crisis will bring an open declaration of war—if not actual conflict.

But before coming to anything so practical as a consideration of what has to be done in view of this huge and impending struggle, let me meet one objection to my general argument which just now occurs to me.

It is said that a state of society which only provides for manual labor and the physical wants of men is disastrous to all higher life and in every way far from desirable; and that to deprive men of the chance of living in "independence" (as it is called) would be to deprive the world of the services of many great thinkers, artists, philanthropists, and benefactors of the human race. Let me say first, and in passing as it were, that if the human masses at large had anything like their rights they would not stand in need of so many philanthropists and benefactors! and that injustice can never in the nature of things grow a greater crop of human welfare and felicity than justice. Secondly, let me say that there is nothing to prevent society from recognising and paying the labor of the artist, the judge, and the thinker even, —as much as it recognises and rewards the labor of the mason and the quarryman; but that this would form no reason for maintaining a vast number of people in abject uselessness and idleness besides. Thirdly, let me say that the production of the necessaries of life *is* still the most important and the foundation element of national life, and that in our present England it is both in honor and in actual pursuit dangerously neglected in favor of the innumerable fancy-work with which it is overlaid. Fourthly, do not let us forget the manifold evils which arise from this so-called "independence"—the waste of life, and its good things, the ennui, unbelief, and ill-health—do not let us forget that this "independent" class is largely responsible for the creation of other classes—such as lawyers, domestic servants, doctors— who if not idle are themselves next to useless to the community, and therefore a burden upon it; and Fifthly, and most important of all, let me remind the reader that if the capitalist class were abolished and a fair share of work at the necessaries of life done by all parties in the nation—the average work so required would be only about three or four hours a day, thus leaving ample time in the remaining hours for other pursuits, and probably causing developments on the intellectual and artistic sides of civilisation hitherto unprecedented and undreamt of.

To proceed now with a consideration of what has

to be done in the immediate future to meet the coming changes. The people are demanding, and will with rapidly increasing loudness demand, that the land of this country and the machinery of industrial production shall be put into the hands of the producers. Under various names, as Nationalisation of the Land, Nationalisation of Capital, Co-operation, Socialism, etc., they will practically demand one thing —namely, that the workers shall directly inherit the fruits of their work, and shall not be mulcted by secondary classes intervening between. The capitalist classes (as a body) will resist this demand; and there will be more or less open war for a considerable period, ending at last no doubt in the deféat of the capitalists. The end cannot really I think be doubtful, but the length of the struggle and the violence of it may depend on a variety of causes. It seems to me in the last degree improbable that any great proportion of the capitalist classes will admit the justice of or yield to the demands of the people; on the contrary, they will organise resistance; and the people will organise attack. And it is only too probable that antagonism will embitter and exaggerate the sense of wrong on both sides. Some few, however, among the capitalist classes will discern the substantial justice of the popular claims, and will have boldness to act up to their convictions; and on the action of these it may greatly depend whether the struggle be ultimately referred to the arbitrament of reason or of force.

In face of the rapidly spreading views (partly explained above) on the nature of rent, interest, and profits, the present attitude of the more well-meaning among the well-to-do classes towards the People seems very inadequate and indeed out of place. It is not patronage and kindly condescension that are required, but mere justice. From the person who has taken from you a large proportion of the fruits of your labor it is not agreeable to receive small doles to keep you from starvation. Charity organisations and unpaid magistracies and the current philanthropic schemes indicate a benevolent intention on the part of those who promote them, but they also indicate an entire misconception as to where the root of the evil lies, and an incapability of realising the way in which the people themselves regard these attempt to remedy it.

On the other hand, perhaps the workers hardly realise how difficult it is for one of the dividend-receiving classes to extricate himself, when he finds his mistake, from the false position into which he has unconsciously got. Trained to no kind of manual work, perhaps to no useful work at all (for of how little real use to the community is the greater part of the work at present done in the select professions!), trained perhaps to no work of any kind, useful or unuseful, he (or she) finds it difficult to satisfy the desire now arising for a clean and faithful life. And indeed, the whole state of society around being unclean and unfaithful, it is difficult for anyone to satisfy that desire.

Yet there are certain lines along which such a person may work with satisfaction—and which I may perhaps try to indicate. In the first place (and perhaps this is as a rule the best plan), remaining in that place or profession in which they are, they may try to make their work in it entirely straightforward and open, and as *useful* to others as possible, especially the poor. This will of course involve losses, monetary and otherwise, and ridicule. But nothing else can be expected or need be wished for. In the second place, to make this course of life feasible and to gradually gain independence from dividends, it will be necessary to reduce expenses greatly, and to adopt a very simple mode of life. The current mode of life among the capitalist people is so needlessly expensive and complex, that few of them, even the more economical, realise how easily it can be simplified, and with how much advantage to health and happiness. But really nowadays the adornments of life, as, for instance, literature, music, art, travel even, are so cheap that very little, after the necessaries have been provided for, is required for the satisfaction of mental wants. A great deal of ignorance no doubt exists among so-called well-to-do people about proper food, and a great deal of unnecessary expense is incurred in this item; but I have not the least doubt—and I am not speaking at random in this matter—that with £120 a year a man and a wife willing to do a fair share of work (and both of them free from any desire to make a pretence of grandeur—for this lies very much at the root of the matter) could bring up a little family in health and happiness—all taking their part in household life—and with education, culture, and refinement equal to any in the land. But such a change as this, or in this direction, at all generally adopted, would enormously alter the aspect of the nation, and bring us nearer to that ideal of social love, justice, and health from which we have so far strayed.

I dwell on these personal reforms first, because surely to each individual they must come first—before any more wide-reaching sphere of usefulness can be reached. Any capitalist or shareholding sort of person who carried out this plan of living would probably after a time find that he (or she) had a considerable balance at the bank to dispose of. He would then have to consider what to do with it. And he would find himself much nearer than before to a practical realisation of the advice which was given on a certain occasion to a young man with great possessions.

Without attempting to limit the directions in which such a person might employ his superfluous possessions, I would suggest that at present the great need of the People (as mentioned above) is to get capital into their own hands for the purpose of employing their own labor. This can only be done by productive Co-operation, either on a small scale, or by the community at large. Anything therefore which will further Co-operation, either by the founding of productive societies, or by a dissemination of ideas on the subject, will I think be especially useful. Furthermore, and beyond this kind of co-operation, something of the nature of National Co-operation is to be aimed at. This practically means Socialism, which I take it is simply the substitution of the rule of general advantage for the rule of individual greed, as represented by Capitalism. The word Socialism, like every new word or idea which comes into the world, carries with it something alarming and offensive. And rightly so. It would be a pity if the angels of the flaming sword did *not* stand at the gate of Paradise —since then every coward and mean humbug could walk in. And if every new stage of human welfare yielded its meaning at once, its conquest would be a little too cheap and easy. Those who view the word from the outside take it to mean confusion, destruction and disorder; and so it does mean (and a good thing that it does) the confusion, destruction and disorder of this old system of living upon other people's labor. But until they have penetrated further than this, outsiders cannot expect to understand the new conception of order and harmony of life which really inspires Socialism and the movement which bears its name.

Behind this word, and giving it authority, stands the huge force of Democracy, the rule of the mass of the people—their interests rather than the interests of the aristocratic or commercial classes. To many serious and thoughtful folk this rule seems full of danger. To them it appears that the working masses, whatever virtues they may have, are essentially disorderly, turbulent, clamorous, and disregardful of rights—and that therefore (as undoubtedly would be the case if this were true) they are, and always must be, unfit—either directly or through representatives— to be the practical rulers of society. I believe myself, however, that this is a complete mistake—a mistake due to ignorance, and to hasty generalisation of those isolated occasions when the people have hitherto forced themselves into notice like volcanic lava through the upper crust of society's indifference and repression. Having had perhaps exceptional opportunities of knowing the various main strata of English social life, I may, without dogmatising on the matter, give it as my decided opinion that the more stable section of the working masses is the real backbone of the nation. My opinion is that this class (if it can be called a class) is in sound sense, orderliness, affectionateness, and wholesome instinct, moral and physical, quite superior to the rest of the nation; that in intellect, if not equal to the detailed work of the scientific people, it has a plain strong mastery derived from its contact with the actual facts of life, which is most if not more important; and that in dealing with moral and political problems it uses a broad sense and tact which often lead it to just conclusions when professional politicians and moralists are floundering among expediencies and casuistries.

Of course the same old blood runs everywhere; and in all sections of social life, as far as I can see, you find the same characters, and differences of character, temperament, passion, and intellect. But, undoubtedly, the habits of life of each class give a special cast and expression to the average underlying humanity. The fashionable, the intellectual, and the commercial classes are each narrowed down in their different ways and along their own lines; that greater class which lives in more direct contact with Nature and the actual facts of life seems to me (notwithstanding the specially trying circumstances of its life in the present day) to be by far the least narrowed, to be by far the most *human;* and I shall always be glad that I have come to know it, as I have done, and to learn some of the best lessons of my life from it.

I do not think, therefore, that in contemplating the changes that are coming upon society, the change from the rule of Capital to the rule of Labor, from Plutocracy to Democracy, from Constitutionalism to Socialism—or whatever you like to call it—we need be alarmed about the upshot or imagine that chaos is before us. For my part I hail the oncoming of this change, and believe that, through whatever struggle and suffering for the time, it will end in the establishment of a far nobler, freer life in the land and in a broader overshadowing of the wings of justice and of peace.

SOCIAL PROGRESS
AND INDIVIDUAL EFFORT.

"The universe could not have been created if God were not a man."—*Swedenborg.*

THE Progress of Society is a subject which occupies much attention nowadays. We hear the shouts and cries of reformers, and are inclined sometimes to be vexed at their noisy insistence and brandishing of panaceas; but when we come to look into the evils to which they draw our attention—under our very noses as it were—and see how serious they are: when we see the misery, the suffering all around us, and see, too, how directly in some cases this appears to be traceable to certain institutions, we can hardly be human if we do not make some effort to alter these institutions and the state of society which goes with them; indeed, at times we feel that it is our highest duty to agitate with the noisiest, and insist at all costs that justice should be done, the iniquity swept away.

And yet on the other hand, when, retiring from the heat and noise of conflict, we mount a little in thought and look out over the world, when we realise —what indeed every day is becoming more abundantly clear—that society is the gigantic growth of centuries, moving on in an irresistible and ordered march of its own, with the precision and fatality of an astronomic orb, how absurd seem all our demonstrations: what an idle beating of the air! The huge beast comes on with elephantine tread. The Liberal sits on his head, and the Conservative sits on his tail; but both are borne along whether they will or no, and both are shaken off before long, inevitably, into the dust. One reformer shouts "This way!" and another shouts "That!" but the great foot comes down and crushes them both, indifferent, crushes the one who thought he was right and the one who found he was wrong, crushes him who would facilitate its progress and him who would stop it, alike.

I confess that I am continually borne about between these two opposing views. On the one hand is Justice, here and now, which must and *shall* be done. On the other hand is Destiny, indifferent, coming down from eternity, which cannot be altered.

Where does the truth lie? Is there any attainable truth in the matter? Perhaps not. The more I think of it, the more am I persuaded that the true explanations, theories, of the social changes which we see around us, that the forces which produce them, that the purposes which they fulfil, lie deep, deep down unsuspected; that the profoundest hitherto science (Buckle, Comte, Marx, Spencer, Morgan, and the rest) has hardly done more than touch the skirt of this great subject. The surface indications, currents, are elusive; the apparent purposes very different from the real ones; individuals, institutions, nations, more or less like puppets or pieces in a game;—the hand that moves them altogether unseen, screening itself effectually from observation.

INDIVIDUAL EFFORT.

Let me take an illustration. You see a young plant springing out of the ground. You are struck by the eager vital growth of it. What elasticity, energy! how it snatches contributions from the winds and sunlight and the earth beneath, and rays itself out with hourly fresh adornment! You become interested to know what is the meaning of all this activity. You watch the plant. It unfolds. The leaf-bud breaks and discloses leaves. These, then, are what it has been aiming at.

But in the axils of the leaves are other leaf-buds, and from these more leaves! The young shoot branches and becomes a little tree or bush. The branching and budding go on, a repetition apparently of one formula. Presently, however, a flower-bud appears. Now we see the real object!

Have you, then, ever carefully examined a flower-bud? Take a rosebud, for instance, or better still perhaps, a dahlia. When quite young the buds of these latter are mere green knobs. Cut one across with your penknife: you will see a green or whitish mass, apparently with but little organisation. Cut another open which is more advanced, and you will see that the traces of structural arrangement have developed, that there are distinct sketches and outlines of what is to follow; later, and your bud will disclose its formation; beneath an outer husk or film —transparent in the case of the dahlia—the petals can already be distinguished, shapen, though not actually separated from each other. Here they lie in block, as it were, conceived yet undelivered, like the statue in the stone, or the thought in the brain of the sculptor. But they are growing momently and expanding. The outermost, or sepals, cohering, form a husk, which for a time protects the young bud. But it also confines it. A struggle ensues, a strangulation, and then the husk gives way, falls off or passes into a secondary place, and the bud opens.

And now the petals uncurl and free themselves like living things to the light. But the process is not finished. Each petal expanding shows another beneath, and these younger ones, as they open, push the older ones outwards, and while these latter are fading there are still new ones appearing in the centre. Envelope after envelope exfoliated—such is the law of life.

At last, however, within the most intimate petals appears the central galaxy—the group of the sexual organs. And now the flower (the petal flower), which just before in all its glory of form, color and fragrance seemed to be the culminating expression and purpose of the plant's life, appears only as a means, an introduction, a secondary thing—a mere advertisement and lure to wandering insects. Within it lies the golden circle of the stamens, the magic staff of the pistil, and the precious ark or *seed-vessel*.

Now then we know what it has all been for, or think we do—for a moment; then we perceive that we are mistaken. For the appearance of the seed-vessel is not the end; it is only a beginning. The flower, the petals, now drop off withered and useless; their work is done. But the seed-vessel begins to swell, to take on structure and form—just as the formless bud did before—there is something at work within. And now it bursts, opens, and falls away. It too

INDIVIDUAL EFFORT. 59

is a husk, and no longer of any importance—for within it appear the *seeds*, the objects of this long toil!

Is the investigation finished? is the process at an end?—No.

Here within this tiny seed lies the promise, the purpose, the vital principle, the law, the inspiration—whatever you like to call it—of this plant's life. Can you find it?

The seed falls to the ground. It swells and takes on form and structure—just as the seed-vessel which enclosed it took on form and structure before—and as the flower-bud (which enclosed the seed-vessel) did before that—and as the leaf-bud (which enclosed the flower-bud) did before that. The seed falls to the ground; it throws off a *husk* (always husks thrown off!)—and discloses an embryo plant—radicle, plumule, and cotyledons—root-shoot, stem-shoot, and seed-leaves—complete. And the circle begins again.

We are baffled after all! We have followed this extraordinary process, we have seen each stage of the plant-growth appearing first as final, and then only as the envelope of a later stage. We have stripped off, so to speak, husk after husk, in our search for the inner secret of the plant-life—we have got down to the tiny seed. But the seed we have found turns out (like every other stage) to be itself only an envelope —to be thrown away in its turn—what we want lies still deeper down. The plant-life begins again—or rather it never ends; but on closer examination we see that that does not repeat itself—it does not move in a circle, but rather in a spiral. The young plant is not the same as the parent, and the next generation varies again from this. When the envelopes have been thrown off a thousand and a hundred thousand times more, a *new form will appear;* will this be a nearer and more perfect expression than before of that within-lying secret—or otherwise ?

To return to society: I began by noting the contrast, often drawn, between the stern, inexorable march of this as a whole, and the equally imperious determination of the individual to interfere with its march—a determination excited by the contemplation of what is called evil, and shapen by an ideal of something better arising within him. Think what a commotion there must be within the bud when the petals of a rose are forming ! Think what arguments, what divisions, what recriminations, even among the atoms, as to which petal they shall join. An organisation has to be constructed and completed. It is finished at last, and a petal is formed. It rays itself out in the sun, is beautiful and unimpeachable for a day; then it fades, is pushed off, its work is done—another from within takes its place.

One social movement succeeds another; the completion of one is the signal for the commencement of the next. Hence there can be no stereotyping: *not to change is to die*—this is the rule of Life; because (and the reason is simple enough) *one* form is not enough to express the secret of life. To express *that* requires an infinite series of forms.

Even a crab cannot get on without changing its shell. It outgrows it. It feels very uncomfortable—pent, sullen, and irritable (much as the bud did before the bursting of the husk, or as society does when dead forms and institutions, generally represented by a class in power, confine its growth)—anxious, too, and oppressed with fears. It—the crab—retires under a rock, out of harm's way, and presently, crack! the shell scales off, and with quietude and patience from within another more suited to it forms. Yet this latter is not final. It is merely the prelude to another.

The feudal arrangement of society succeeded the clannish and patriarchal, the commercial or competitive system succeeds the feudal, the socialistic succeeds the commercial, and the socialistic is succeeded in its turn by other stages; and each of these includes numerous minor developments. The politician or reformer who regards any of these stages or steps as containing the whole secret and redemption of society commits just the same mistake as the theologian who looks upon any one doctrine as necessary to salvation. He is betrayed into the most frightful harshness, narrow-mindedness, and intolerance—and if he has power will become a tyrant. Just the same danger has to be guarded against by everyone of us in daily life. Who is there who (though his reason may contend against it) does not drop into the habit of regarding some one change in his life and surroundings as containing finally the secret of his happiness, and excited by this immense prospect, does not do things which he afterwards regrets, and which end in disappointment? There is a millennium, but it does not belong to any system of society that can be named, nor to any doctrine, belief, circumstance, or surrounding of individual life. The secret of the plant-life does not tarry in any one phase of its growth; it eludes from one phase to another, still lying within and within the latest. It is within the grain of mustard seed: it is so small. Yet it rules and is the purpose of every stage, and is like the little leaven which, invisible in three measures of meal, yet leavened the whole lump.

Of the tendency, of which I have spoken, of social forms to stereotype themselves, Law is the most important and in some sense the most pernicious instance. Social progress is a continual fight against it. Popular customs get hardened into laws. Even thus they soon constitute evils. But in the more complex stages of society, when classes arise, the law-making is generally in the hands of a class, and the laws are hardened (often very hardened) class practices. These shells have to be thrown off and got rid of at all costs —or rather they *will* inevitably be thrown off when the growing life of the people underneath forces this liberation. It is a bad sign when a patient, "law-abiding" people submit like sheep to old forms which are really long out-worn. "Where the men and women think lightly of the laws . . . there the great city stands," says Walt Whitman.

I remember once meeting with a pamphlet written by an Italian, whose name I have forgotten, member of a secularist society, to prove that the Devil was the author of all human progress. Of course that, in his sense, is true. The spirit of opposition to established order, the war against the continuance (as a finality) of any institution or order, however good it may be for the time, is a necessary element of

social progress, is a condition of the very life of
society. Without this it would die.

Law is a strangulation. Yet while it figures constantly as an evil in social life, it must not therefore
be imagined to be bad or without use. On the contrary, its very appearance as an evil is part of its use.
It is the husk which protects and strengthens the bud
while it confines it. Possibly the very confinement
and forcible repression which it exercises is one element in the more rapid organisation of the bud within. It is the crab's shell which gives form and
stability to the body of the creature, but which has
to give way when a more extended form is wanted.

In the present day in modern society the strangulation of the growth of the people is effected by the
capitalist class. This class together with its laws and
institutions constitutes the husk which has to be
thrown off just as itself threw off the husk of the
feudal aristocracy in its time. The commercial and
capitalist envelope has undoubtedly served to protect
and give form to (and even nourish) the growing life
of the people. But now its function in that respect
is virtually at an end. It appears merely as an
obstacle and an evil—and will inevitably be removed,
either by a violent disruption or possibly by a
gradual absorption into the socialised proletariat beneath.

At all times, and from whatever points of view, it
should be borne in mind that laws are made by the
people, not the people by the laws. Modern European
society is cumbered by such a huge and complicated
overgrowth of law, that the notion actually gets

abroad that such machinery is necessary to keep the people in order—that without it the mass of the people would not live an orderly life; whereas all observation of the habits of primitive and savage tribes, destitute of laws, and almost destitute of any authoritative institutions—and all observation of the habits of civilised people when freed from law (as in gold-mining and other backwood communities)—show just the reverse. The instinct of man is to an orderly life, the law is but the result and expression of this. As well attribute the organisation of a crab to the influence of its shell, as attribute the orderly life of a nation to the action of its laws. Law *has* a purpose and an influence—but the idea that it is to preserve order is elusive. All its machinery of police and prisons do not, cannot do this. At best in this sense it only preserves an order advantageous to a certain class; it is the weapon of a slow and deliberate warfare. It springs from hatred and rouses opposition, and so has a healthy influence.

Fichte said: "The object of all government is to render government superfluous." And certainly if external authority of any kind has a final purpose, it must be to establish and consolidate an internal authority. Whitman adds to his description of "the great city," that it stands "where outside authority enters always after the precedence of inside authority." When this process is complete, government in the ordinary sense is already "rendered superfluous." Anyhow this external governmental power is obviously self-destructive. It has no permanence or finality about it, but in every period of history appears as a husk

INDIVIDUAL EFFORT.   65

or snell preparing the force within which is to reject it.

Thus I have in a very fragmentary and imperfect way called attention to some general conditions of social progress, conditions by which the growth of society is probably comparable with the growth of a plant, or an animal, or an astronomic organism, subject to laws and an order of its own, in face of which the individual would at first sight appear to count as nothing. But there is, as usual, a counter-truth which must not be overlooked. If society moves by an ordered and irresistible march of its own, so also—as a part of society, and beyond that as a part of Nature—does the individual. In his right place, the individual is also irresistible.

Now then, when you have seized your life-inspiration, your absolute determination, *you* also are irresistible, the whole weight of this vast force is behind you. Huge as the institutions of society are, vast as is the sweep of its traditions and customs, yet in face of it all, the word "I will" is not out of place.

Let us take the law of the competitive struggle for existence—which has been looked upon by Political Economists (perhaps with some justice) as the base of social life. It is often pointed out that this law of competition rules throughout the animal and vegetable kingdoms as well as through the region of human society, and therefore, it is said, being evidently a universal law of Nature, it is useless and hopeless to expect that society can ever be founded on any other basis. Yet I say that granting this assumption—and in reality the same illusion underlies the application of the word "law" here, as we saw before in its social application—granting, I say that competition has hitherto been the universal law, the last word, of Nature, still if only one man should stand up and say, "It shall be so no more," if he should say, "It is not the last word of *my* nature, and my acts and life declare that it is not,"—then that so-called law would be at an end. He being a part of Nature has as much right to speak as any other part, and as in the elementary law of hydrostatics a slender column of water can balance (being at the same height) against an ocean—so his Will (if he understand it aright) can balance all that can be arrayed against him. If only one man—with regard to social matters—speaking from the very depth of his heart says, "This shall not be: behold something better;" his word is likely stronger than all institutions, all traditions. And why?—because in the deeps of his individual heart he touches also that of society, of man. Within himself, in quiet, he has beheld the secret, he has seen a fresh crown of petals, a golden circle of stamens, folded and slumbering in the bud. Man forms society, its laws and institutions, and man can reform them. Somewhere within yourself, be assured, the secret of that authority lies.

The fatal words spoken by individuals—the words of progress—are provoked by what is called *evil*. Every human institution is good in its time, and then becomes evil—yet it may be doubted whether it is really evil in itself, but rather because if it remained it would hinder the next step. Each petal is pushed out by the next one. A new growth of the moral sense takes place first within the individual—and this gives birth to a new ideal, something to love better than anything seen before. Then in the light of this new love, this more perfect desire, what has gone before and the actually existing things appear wizened and *false* (*i.e.*, ready to *fall* like the petals). They become something to hate, they are evil; and the perception of evil is already the promise of something better.

Do not be misled so as to suppose that science and the intellect are or can be the sources of social progress or change. It is the moral births and outgrowths that originate; science and the intellect only give form to these. It is a common notion and one apparently gaining ground, that science may, as it were, take society by the hand and become its high priest and guide to a glorious kingdom. And this to a certain extent is true. Science may become high-priest, but the result of its priestly offices will entirely depend on what kind of deity it represents—what kind of god society worships. Science will doubtless become its guide, but whither it leads society will entirely depend on whither society desires to be led. If society worships a god of selfish curiosity, the holy rites and priesthood of science will consist in vivisection and the torture of the loving animals; if society believes above all things in material results, science will before long provide these things,—it will surround men with machinery and machine-made products, it will whirl them about ("behind steam-kettles," as Mr. Ruskin says) from one end of the world to the other, it will lap them in every luxury and debility, and give

them fifty thousand toys to play with, where before
they had only one—but through all the whistling of
the kettles and the rattling of the toys it will not
make the still small voice of God sound nearer. If
society, in short, worships the Devil, science will lead
it to the Devil; and if society worships God, science
will open up and clear away much that encumbered
the path to God. (And here I use these terms, as
lawyers say, "without prejudice.") No mere scientific adjustments will bring about the millennium.
Granted that the problem is Happiness, there must be
certain moral elements in the mass of mankind before
they will even *desire* that kind of happiness which is
attainable, let alone their capacity of reaching it;—
when these moral elements are present, the intellectual or scientific solution of the problem will be
soon found; without them there will not really be any
serious attempt made to find it. That is—as I said
at the head of this paragraph—science and the intellect are not, and never can be, the sources of social
progress and change. It is the moral births and outgrowths that originate; the intellect stands in a
secondary place as the tool and instrument of the
moral faculty.

The commercial and competitive state of society
may be taken to indicate an upheaval from the feudal
of a new (and perhaps grander) sentiment of human
right and dignity. Arising simultaneously with
Protestantism it meant—they both meant—individualism, the assertion of man's worth and dignity as man,
and as against any feudal lordship or priestly hier-
archy. It was an outburst of feeling first. It was

the sense of equality spreading. It took the form of individualism—the equality of rights—Protestantism in religion, competition in commerce. It resulted in the social emancipation of a large class, the *bourgeoisie*. Feudalism, now dwindled to a husk, was thrown off; and for a time the glory, the life of society was in the new order.

But to-day a wider claim, or at least a fresh impulse towards humanity, asserts itself. Competition in setting itself up as the symbol of human equality, was (like all earthly representations of what is divine) only an imperfect symbol. It had the elements of mortality and dissolution in it. For while it destroyed the privilege of rank and emancipated a huge class, it ended after all by enslaving another class and creating the privilege of wealth. Competition, in fact, represented a portion of human equality, but not the whole: insisting on individual rights all round, it overlooked the law of charity, turned sour with the acid of selfishness, and became as to-day the gospel of "the devil take the hindmost." Arising glorious as the opponent of iniquity in high places, it has ended by denying the very source from whence it sprung. Like many a popular hero it has turned tyrant, and must share the tyrant's doom.

Competition is doomed. Once a good, it has now become an evil. But simultaneously (and probably as part of the same process) springs up, as I say, a new ethical conception. Everywhere to-day signs of this may be seen, felt. It is *felt* that the relation which systematically allows the weaker to go to the wall is not human. Individualism, the mere separate pursuit, each of his own good, on the basis of equality, does not satisfy the heart. The *right* (undoubted though it may be) to take advantage of another's weakness or inferiority, does not please us any longer. Science and the intellect have nothing to say to this, for or against,—they can merely stand and look on—arguments may be brought on both sides. What I say is that as a fact a change is taking place in the general sentiment in this matter; some deeper feeling of human solidarity, brotherliness, charity, some more genuine and substantial apprehension of the meaning of the word equality, is arising—some broader and more determined sense of justice. Though making itself felt as yet only here and there, still there are indications that this new sentiment is spreading; and if it becomes anything like general, then inevitably (I say) it will bring a new state of society with it— will be in fact such new state of society.

When talking one day about the current Political Economy with William Smith (author of "Thorndale," etc.), he said: "They assume self-interest as the one guiding principle of human nature, and so make it the basis of their science—but even if it is so now, it may not always be so, and the change of basis would entirely re-model their science." The speaker was at the time quite an invalid—on his death-bed it might be said; and I do not know that he was even aware that a new school of political economy with some such changed basis—the school of Marx, Engels, Lassalle and others—was then in existence. But, whether aware or not, I contend that this dying man—even if he had been alone in the world in his aspiration—

feeling within himself a deeper, more intimate principle of action than that expressed in the existing state of society, might have been confident that at some time or other—if not immediately—it would come to the surface and find its due interpretation and translation in a new order of things. And I contend that whoever to-day feels that there is a better standard of life than the higgling of the market, and a juster scale of wages than "what A or B will *take*," and a more important question in an undertaking than "how much per cent. it will pay"—contains or conceals *in himself* the germs of a new social order.

Socialism, if that is to be the name of the next wave of social life, springs from and demands as its basis a new sentiment of humanity, a better sort of morality. That is the essential part of it. A science it is, but only secondarily; for we must remember that as the *bourgeois* political economy sprang from certain moral data, so the socialist political economy implies other moral data. Both are right enough on their own axioms. And when these axioms in course of time change again (as they infallibly will) another science of political economy, doubtless, will spring up, and socialist political economy will be false.

The morality being the essential part of the movement, it is important to keep that in view. If Socialism, as Mr. Matthew Arnold has pointed out, means merely a change of society without a change of its heart—if it merely means that those who grabbed all the good things before shall be displaced, and that those who were grabbed from should now grab in their turn—it amounts to nothing, and is not in effect

a change at all, except quite upon the surface. If it
is to be a substantial movement, it must mean a
changed ideal, a changed conception of daily life; it
must mean some better conception of human dignity
—such as shall scorn to claim anything for its own
which has not been duly earned, and such as shall not
find itself degraded by the doing of any work, however menial, which is useful to society; it must mean
simplicity of life, defence of the weak, courage of
one's own convictions, charity of the faults and fail-
ings of others. These things first and a larger slice of
pudding all round afterwards!

How can such morality be spread?—How does a
plant grow?—It *grows*. There is some contagion of
influence in these matters. Knowledge can be taught
directly; but a new ideal, a new sentiment of life,
can only pass by some indirect influence from one to
another. Yet it does pass. There is no need to talk
—perhaps the less said in any case about these
matters the better—but if you have such new ideal
within you, it is I believe, your clearest duty, as well
as your best interest, to act it out in your own life.
Then we must not forget that a wise order of society
once established (by the strenuous action of a few)
reacts on its members. To a certain extent it is true,
perhaps, that men and women can be *grown*—like
cabbages. And this is a case of the indirect influence
of the strenuous few upon the many.

Thus—in this matter of society's change and progress—(though I feel that the subject as a whole is
far too deep for me)—I do think that the birth of new
moral conceptions in the individual is at least a very

important factor. It may be in one individual or in a hundred thousand. As a rule, probably, when one man feels any such impulse strongly, the hundred thousand are nearer to him than he suspects. (When one leaf, or petal, or stamen begins to form on a tree, or one plant begins to push its way above the ground in spring, there are hundreds of thousands all round just ready to form.) Anyhow, whether he is alone or not, the new moral birth is sacred—as sacred as the child within the mother's womb—it is a kind of blasphemy against the Holy Ghost to conceal it. And when I use the word "moral" here—or anywhere above—I do not, I hope, mean that dull pinch-lipped conventionality of negations which often goes under that name. The deep-lying ineradicable desires, fountains of human action, the life-long aspirations, the lightning-like revelations of right and justice, the treasured hidden ideals, born in flame and in darkness, in joy and sorrow, in tears and in triumph, within the heart—are, as a rule, anything but conventional. They may be, and often are, thought *im*moral. I don't care, they are sacred just the same. If they underlie a man's life, and are nearest to himself—they will underlie humanity. " To your own self be true. . . ."

Anyhow courage is better than conventionality: take your stand and let the world come round to you. Do not think you are right and everybody else wrong. If you think you are wrong then you may be right; but if you think you are right then you are certainly wrong. Your deepest, highest moral conceptions are only for a time. They have to give place. They are the envelopes of freedom—that eternal freedom which cannot be represented—that peace which passes understanding. Somewhere here is the invisible vital principle, the seed within the seed. It may be held but not thought, felt but not represented—except by life and history. Every individual so far as he touches this stands at the source of social progress—behind the screen on which the phantasmagoria play.

DESIRABLE MANSIONS.

"The Widow Douglas, she took me for her son, and allowed she would civilise me; but it was rough living in the house all the time, considering how dismal regular and decent the widow was in all her ways; and so when I couldn't stand it no longer I lit out."—*Mark Twain.*

AFTER all, why should we rail against the rich? I think if anything they should be pitied. In nine cases out of ten it is not a man's fault. He is born in the lap of luxury, he grows up surrounded by absurd and impossible ideas about life, the innumerable chains of habit and circumstance tighten upon him, and when the time comes that he would escape, he finds he cannot. He is condemned to flop up and down in his cage for the remainder of his days—a spectacle of boredom, and a warning to gods and men.

I go into the houses of the rich. In the drawing-room I see chill weary faces, peaked features of ill-health; downstairs and in the kitchen I meet with rosy smiles, kissable cheeks, and hear sounds of song and laughter. What is this? Is it possible that the real human beings live with James below-stairs!

Often as I pass and see in suburb or country some "desirable mansion" rising from the ground, I think: That man is building a prison for himself. So it is—

a prison. I would rather spend a calendar month in Clerkenwell or Holloway than I would in that desirable mansion. A young lady that I knew, and who lived in such a mansion, used with her sisters to teach a class of factory girls. Every now and again one of the girls would say, " Eh, Miss, how I would like to be a grand lady like you ! " Then she would answer, " Yes, but you wouldn't be able to do everything you liked ; for instance, you wouldn't be allowed to go out walking when you liked." " Eh, dear ! " they would say to one another, " she is not allowed to go out walking when she likes—she is not allowed to go out walking when she likes ! "

Certainly you are not allowed to go out walking when you like. Sometimes it is my lot to have to spend a day within those desirable walls. I wake up in the morning. It is fine and bright. I think to myself : I will have a pleasant stroll before breakfast. Yes—man proposes. It is all very well to meditate a morning walk, but where O where are my clothes ? I cannot very well go out without them. What can have become of them ? Suddenly it occurs to me : James, honest soul, has taken them away to brush. Good. I wait. Nothing happens. I ring the bell. James appears. " My clothes, James." " Yes, sir." Again I wait—an intolerable time. At last the familiar jacket and trousers appear. Good. Now I can go out. Not so fast—where are your boots ? Boots, good gracious, I had forgotten them. Heaven knows where they are—I don't. Probably fifty yards away. I creep downstairs. All is quiet. The servants are evidently at breakfast. It would be madness to hope to get boots brushed at such a moment. I would like to clean them myself. In fact I am fond of cleaning my own boots; the exertion is not unpleasant, and besides it is just such a little bit of menial work as I would rather do for myself than have others do for me; but, as I said before, one cannot do what one likes. In the first place, in this house where one is fifty yards away from everything one wants, I have not the faintest idea where my boots are, or the means and instruments of blacking them; in the second place an even more fatal objection is that if I did succeed in committing this deed of darkness the consequences would be quite indescribable. The outrage on propriety would not only shock the feelings of the world below stairs, but it would put to confusion the master of the house, upset the domestic machinery, create unpleasant qualms in the minds of the other guests, and possibly make me feel that I had better not have lived. Accordingly I abandon the idea of my pleasant stroll. It is not worth such a sacrifice. The birds are singing outside, the flowers are gay in the morning sun—but it must not be. Within, in the sitting-rooms, chaos reigns. Chairs and tables are piled in cheerful confusion upon one another, carpets are partially strewn with tea-leaves. To read a book or write an aimless letter to someone (the usual resource of people in desirable mansions) is clearly impossible; to do anything in the way of house-work is forbidden—it being well understood in such places that one may do anything *except what is useful*. There remains nothing but to beat a retreat to my chamber again—put my hands in my pockets and whistle at the open window.

"Who was that I heard whistling so early this morning?" says my kindly old host at breakfast. "O, it was you, was it? I expect now you're an early riser; get up at seven, take a walk before breakfast; that sort of thing—eh?" "Yes, when I can," I reply with ambiguous intent. "Well, I call that wonderful," says an elderly matron—not likely, as far as appearances go, to be accused of a similar practice—"such energy, you know." "*What* a strong constitution you must have to be able to stand it!" remarks a charming young lady on whom it has not yet dawned that the vast majority of human kind have their breakfast before half-past nine.

This is not a good beginning to the day; but the rest is like unto it. I find that there are certain things to be done—a certain code of things that you may do, a certain way of doing them, a certain way of putting your knife and fork on your plate. When you come down to dinner in the evening you must put on what the Yankees call a claw-hammer coat. It is not certain (and that is just the grisly part of it) *what* would happen if you did not do this. In some societies evidently such a casualty has never been contemplated. I have heard people seriously discussing—in cases where the required article was missing—what could be done, where one might be borrowed, etc.—but clearly it did not occur to them that anyone could dine in his natural clothes. Sometimes, when in a fashionable church, I have wondered whether it would be possible to worship God in a flannel shirt—but I suppose that to go out to a dinner-party in such a costume would be even more unthinkable. As I said before, you are in prison. Submit to the prison rules, and it is all right—attempt to go beyond them, and you are visited with condign punishment. The rules have no sense, but that does not matter (possibly some of them had sense once, but it must have been a very long time ago); the people are good people, no better nor worse in themselves than the real workers, the real hands and hearts of the world; but they are condemned to banishment from the world, condemned into the prison-houses of futility. The stream of human life goes past them as they gaze wearily upon it through their plate-glass windows; the great mother's breasts of our common Humanity are withheld from them. Dimly at last I think I understand why it is their faces are so chill and sad, their unnourished lives so unhealthy and over-sensitive. Truly, if I could pity anyone, I would them.

By the side of the road there stands a little girl crying; she has lost her way. It is very cold, and she looks pinched and starved. "Come in, my little girl, and sit by my cottage fire, and you'll soon get warm; and I'll see if I can't find you a bit of something to eat before you go on. . . . Eh! dear! how stupid I am—I quite forgot. I am sorry I can't ask you in, but I am living in a desirable mansion now—and though we are *very* sorry for you, yet you see we could hardly have you into our house, for your dirty little boots would make a dreadful mess of our carpets, and we should have to dust the chairs after you had sat upon them, and you see Mrs. Vavasour might happen to come in, and she would think it so very *odd;* and I know cook can't bear beggars, and, O dear! I'm so sorry for you—and here's a penny, and I hope you'll get home safely."

The stream of human life goes past. When a rich man builds himself a prison, he puts up all these fences to shut the world out—to shut himself in. If he can he builds far back from the high road. In the front of his house he has a boundless polite lawn, with polite flower-beds, afar from vulgar people and animals. Rows of polite servants attend upon him; and there, within, of inanity and politeness he dies. Of what human life really consists in he has little idea. Sometimes with an indistinct vision of accumulated evil, he says: "Poor So-and-so, he has only £200 a year to keep his wife and family on!" No wonder his own daughters dedicate themselves to "good works." They go out under the curate's instruction and visit at neighboring cottages. Their visits have little appreciable effect on the people, but are a great benefit to themselves and the curate. They observe, for the first time, how life is carried on; they see the operations of scrubbing and cooking (removed in their own houses afar from mortal polite eye); perhaps they behold a mother actually suckling her own babe, and learn that such things are possible; finally, they "wonder" how "those people" live, and to them their wonder (like the fear of God) is the beginning of wisdom. The lord of the mansion sits on the magisterial bench, or strides about his fields, and lumps together all who are not in a similar position to himself as the "lower classes." After dinner in the evening, if the conversation turns on politics, he and his compeers discuss the importance of keeping the said lower classes in order, or the best method of "raising" them out of the ignorance and disorder in which they are supposed to wallow. And during the conversation it will be noticed that it is by everyone tacitly allowed and understood, and is, in fact, the very foundation of the whole argument, that the speakers themselves belong to an educated class, while the mass of the people are uneducated. Yet this is exactly the reverse of the truth—for they themselves belong to an ill-educated class, and the mass of the people are, by the very nature of the case, the better educated of the two.

In fact, the education of the one set of people (and it is a great pity that it should be so) consists almost entirely in the study of books. That is very useful in its way, and if properly balanced with other things; but it is hardly necessary to point out that books only deal with phantoms and shadows of reality. The education of the world at large, and the real education, lies, and must always lie, in dealing with the things themselves. To put it shortly (as it has been put before), one man learns to spell a "spade," to write it, to rhyme it, to translate it into French and Latin—possibly, like Wordsworth, to address a sonnet to it—the other man learns to *use* it. Is there any comparison between the two? Now is it not curious that those good people sitting round their dinner-table in the desirable mansion, or listening to a little music in the drawing-room, should actually be so ignorant of the world, and what goes on in it, as to think, and honestly believe, that *they are, par ex. cellence,* the educated people in it?[1] Does it ever occur to them, I often think, to inquire who made all the elegant and costly objects with which they are surrounded? Does it ever occur to them, as they tacitly assume the inferiority of the working classes, to think of the table itself across which they speak— how beautifully fitted, veneered, polished; the cloth which lies upon it, and the weaving of it; the chairs and other furniture, so light and yet so strong, each requiring the skill of years to make; the silver, the glass, the steel, the tempering, hardening, grinding, fitting, riveting; the lace and damask curtains, the wonderful machinery, the care, the delicate touch, adroit manipulation; the piano! the very house itself wherein they spend their days! Is there one, I say, who we will not say could make even the smallest part, but who even has the faintest idea how one of these things is made, where it is made, who makes it? Not one. All the care, the loving thought, the artistic design, the conscientious workmanship that have been expended, and are daily expended, on these things and the like of them—go past these folk unrecognised,

[1] " . . . . People who roll about in their fine equipages scarcely knowing what to do with themselves or what ails them, and some of whom occasionally run to such places as ours to have their carriage linings or cushions altered, or to know if they *can* be altered, as *they don't feel quite comfortable.* I often think ' God help them,' for no one else can. . . ."

I insert this extract just to show how these things are regarded from the side which does not usually find expression. It is from a letter written by an elderly and gentle-hearted man employed in a carriage factory.

unacknowledged. The great hymn of human labor over the earth is to them an idle song. There, in the midst of all these beautiful products of toil and ingenuity, possessing but not enjoying, futile they sit, and fancy themselves educated—fit to rule. I have heard of a fly that sat stinging upon the hind-quarters of a horse, and fancied that without it the cart would not go. Fancied so, I say, until the great beast whisked its tail, and after that it fancied nothing more.

Do I put these things in a strong light? May be I do; but I put them faithfully as I have seen them, and as I see them daily. I do not suppose that riches are an evil in themselves. I do not suppose that anything is an evil in itself. I know that even in the midst of all these shackles and impediments, that wonderfulest of things, the human soul, may work out its own salvation; and well I know that there are no conditions or circumstances of human life, nor any profession from a king to a prostitute, that may not become to it the gateway of freedom and immortality. But I daily see people setting this standard of well-to-do respectability before them, daily more and more hastening forth in quest of desirable mansions to dwell in; and I cannot but wonder whether they realise *what* it is they seek; I cannot lend my voice to swell the chorus of encouragement. Here are the clean facts. Choose for yourselves. That is all.

Respectability! Heavy-browed and hunch-backed word. Once innocent and light-hearted as any other word, why now in thy middle age art thou become so gloomy and saturnine? *Is it that thou art re-*

sponsible for the murder of the innocents? Respectability! Vision of clean hands and blameless dress—why dost thou now appear in the form of a ghoul before me?

I confess that the sight of a dirty hand is dear to me. It warms my heart with all manner of good hopes and promises. Often have I thought about this matter, and in all good faith I must say that I fail to see how hands always clean are compatible with honesty. This is no play upon words. I fail to see how in the long run, any man that takes his share in the work of the world can keep his hands in this desirable state.

How? The answer is obvious enough—leave others to do the dirty work. Good! Let it be so; let it be granted that others shall do the scrubbing and baking, the digging, the fishing, the breaking of horses, the carpentering, building, smithing, and the myriad other jobs that have to be done, and you at the pinnacle of all this pyramid of work, above all, keep your hands clean. We shouting to you from below, exhort you—At all costs, keep your hands clean! Think how important it is, while the great ships have to be got into harbor, that *your* nails should be blameless! Think if by any accident you were to do a real good piece of work, and get your hands thoroughly grimed over it, unwashable for a week, what confusion would ensue to yourself and friends! Think, O think, of your clients, or of the next dinner-party, and earnestly and prayerfully resolve that such a fall may never be yours. Seek, we pray you, some secure work—some legal, clerical, official, capitalist, or land-owning business, safe from the dread stain of dirty hands, whatever other dirt it may bring with it—some thoroughly gentlemanly profession, marking you clearly off from the vulgar and general masses, and the blessing of heaven go with you!

Shut yourself off from the great stream of human life, from the great sources of physical and moral health; ignore the common labor by which you live, show clearly your contempt for it, your dislike of it, and then ask others to do it for you; turn aside from nature, divorce yourself from the living, breathing heart of the nation; and then you will have done what the governing classes of England to-day have done, have given full directions to your own heart and brain how to shrivel and starve and die.

Man is made to work with his hands. This is a fact which cannot be got over. From this central fact he cannot travel far. I don't care whether it is an individual or a class, the life which is far removed from this becomes corrupt, shrivelled, and diseased. You may explain it how you like, but it is so. Administrative work has to be done in a nation as well as productive work; but it must be done by men accustomed to manual labor, who have the healthy decision and primitive authentic judgment which comes of that, else it cannot be done well. In the new form of society which is slowly advancing upon us, this will be felt more than now. The higher the position of trust a man occupies, the more will it be thought important that, at some period of his life, he should have been thoroughly inured to manual work;

this not only on account of the physical and moral robustness implied by it, but equally because it will be seen to be impossible for anyone, without this experience of what is the very flesh and blood of national life, to promote the good health of the nation, or to understand the conditions under which the people live whom he has to serve.

But to return to the sorrows of the well-to-do—and care that sits on the crupper of wealth. This is a world-old and well-worn subject. Yet, possibly, some of its truisms may bear repeating. A clergyman, preaching once on the trials of life, turned first to his rich friends and bade them call to mind, one by one, the sorrows and sufferings of the poor; then, turning to his "poorer brethren," he exhorted them also not to forget that the rich man had his afflictions—with which they should sympathise—amongst which afflictions, growing chiefly out of their much money, he reckoned "last, but not least, the difficulty of finding for it an investment which should be profitable and *also secure!*" It has been generally supposed that the poorer brethren failed to sympathise with this form of suffering.

But it is a very real one. What cares, what anxieties, what yellow and blue fits, what sleepless nights, dance attendance on the worshiper in the great Temple of Stocks! The capricious deity that dwells there has to be appeased by ceaseless offerings. Usury! crookfaced idol, loathed, yet grovelled to by half the world, whose name is an abomination to speak openly, yet whose secret rites are practised by thousands who revile thy name, what spell of gloom and bilious misery dost thou cast over thy worshipers! Is it possible that the ancient curse has not yet lost its effect: that to acquire interest on money and to acquire interest in life are *not* the same thing; that they are positively not compatible with each other; that to fiy from one's just share of labor in the world, in order to live upon the hard-earned profits of others, is not, and cannot come to good? Is it possible, I say, reader, that there *is* a moral law in the world facing us quite calmly in every transaction of our lives by which it must be so—by which cowardice and sham cannot breed anything else for us but gloom and bilious misery? In this age which rushes to stocks—to debenture, preference, consolidated, and ordinary stocks, to shares, bonds, coupons, dividends—not even refusing scrip when it can get it—does it ever occur to us to consider what it all means?—to consider that all the money so gained is *taken* from someone else; that what we have not *earned* cannot possibly be ours, except by gift, or (putting it plainly) *theft?* How can it then come to good for us? How can we not but think of the railway operatives, the porters, managers, clerks, superintendents, drivers, stokers, platelayers, carriage-washers, navvies, out of whose just earnings (and from no other source) our dividends are taken? Let alone honesty—what, surely, does our pride say to this? Is it possible that this frantic dividend-dance of the present day is like a dance of dancers dancing without any music—an aimless, incoherent, impossible dance, weltering down at last to idiocy and oblivion?

Curious, is it not, that this subject (of dividends) is

never mentioned before said wage-receiving classes? One may often notice that. When James enters the room, or Jeffery comes to look at the gas-fittings, the babble of stocks dies faintly away, as if ashamed of itself; and while a man will, without reserve, allude to his professional salary, he is generally as secret concerning his share-gotten gains as ladies are said to be about their age.

But, as I said at first, these things are not altogether a man's fault. They are the product of the circumstances in which he is born. From his childhood he is trained ostensibly in the fear of God, but really in the fear of Money. The whole tenor of the conversation which he hears round him, and his early teaching, tend to impress upon him the awful dangers of not having *enough*. Strange that it never occurs to parents of this class to teach their children how *little* they can live upon, and be well off (but perhaps they do not know). Dark hints of the workhouse are whispered in the boy's ears; father and mother, school-teachers and friends, join in pressing him into a profession which he hates—stultifying his whole life—because it will lead to £500, or even £1,000 a year in course of time. This is the great test, the sure criterion between two paths: which will lead to more money? The youthful tender conscience soon comes to look upon it as a duty, and the acquisition of large dividends as part of the serious work of life. Then come true the words of the preacher: he realises with painful clearness the difficulty of finding investments which shall be profitable and *also secure;* circulars, reports, newspaper-cuttings, and warning letters, flow

in upon him; sleepless nights are followed by anxious
days; telegrams and railway journeys succeed each
other But the game goes on: the income gets bigger,
and the fear of the workhouse looms closer ! Friends.
and relations also have shares. Some get married
and others die. Hence trusteeships and executor-
ships, increasing in number year by year, coil upon
coil; solicitors hover around on all sides, jungles of
legal red tape have to be waded through, chancery
looms up with its "obscene birds" upon the horizon,
and the hapless boy, now an old man before his time,
with snatched meals and care-lined brow, goes to and
fro like an automaton—a walking testimony to his
own words that "the days of his happiness are long
gone past." By all the gods, I would rather with
pick and shovel dig a yearlong drain beneath the
open sky, breathing freely, than I would live in this
jungle of idiotic duties and thin-lipped respectabilities
that money breeds. Why the devil should the days
of your happiness be gone past, except that you have
lived a life to stultify the whole natural man in you ?
Do you think that happiness is a little flash-in-the-
pan when you are eighteen, and that is all ? Do you
not know that expanding age, like a flower, lifts itself
ever into a more and more exquisite sunlight of
happiness, to which Death, serene and beautiful,
comes only at the last with the touch of perfected
assurance ? Do you not know that the whole effort
of Nature in you is towards this happiness, if you
could only abandon yourself, and for one child-like
moment have faith in your own mother ? But she
knows it, and, half-amused, watches you run after

your little "securities," knowing surely that you must at length return to her.

Another matter wherein the affluent classes suffer much in the present day is that of health. If there is one thing that appears to me more certain than another it is, as I have partly said before, that no individual or class can travel far from the native life of the race without becoming shrivelled, corrupt, diseased —without suffering, in fact. By the native life I mean the life of those (always the vast majority of human kind) who live and support themselves in direct contact with Nature.[1] To rise early, to be mostly in the open air, to do some amount of physical labor, to eat clean and simple food, are necessary and aboriginal conditions of the life of our race, and they are necessary and aboriginal conditions of health. The doctor who does not start from these as the basis of his prescriptions does not know his work. The modern money-lender, man of stocks, or whatever you call him, and his family, live in the continual violation of these conditions. They get up late, are mostly

[1] I do not mean here to imply that the working masses of our great towns by any means fulfil this condition. In fact it is notorious that their health is even worse than that of the wealthy classes. Thrust down into squalor by the very effort of others climbing to luxury, the unnaturalness and misery of their lives is the direct counterpart and inseparable accompaniment of the unnaturalness of the lives of the rich. That the great masses of our population to-day are in this unhealthy state does not however disprove the statement in the text—*i.e.*, that the vast majority of mankind must live in direct contact with Nature —rather it would indicate that the present conditions can only be of brief duration.

indoors, do little or no physical work, and take quantities of rich and greasy food and stimulants, such as would overburden the stomach even of a strong man. Hence a long catalogue of evils, ever branching into more, and especially noticeable among the womenkind. Hence dyspepsia, nerves, liver, sexual degeneracies, and general depression of vitality; a gloomy train, but whose drawn features you will recognise if you peep into almost any one of those desirable mansions of which I have spoken. A terrible symptom of our well-to-do (?) modern life is this want of health, and one which presses for serious attention. There is only one remedy for it; but that remedy is a sure one— the return (or advance) to a squarer, truer, more natural mode of existence.

What is the upshot of all this? There was a time when the rich man had duties attending his wealth. The lord or baron was a petty king, and had kingly responsibilities as well as power. The Sir Roger, of Addison's time, was the succeeding type of landlord. And even to the present day there lingers here and there a country squire who fulfils that now antiquated ideal of kindly condescension and patronage. But the modern rush of steam-engines, and the creation of an enormous class of wealthy folk living on stocks, have completely subverted the old order. It has let loose on society a horde of wolves!—a horde of people who have no duties attaching to their mode of life, no responsibility. They roam hither and thither, seeking whom and what they may devour. Personally I have no objection to criminals, and think them quite as good as myself. But, Talk of criminal classes—can there be a doubt that *the* criminal classes in our modern society are this horde of stock and share-mongers? If to be a criminal is to be an enemy of society, then they are such. For their mode of life is founded on the principle of taking without giving, of claiming without earning—as much as that of any common thief. It is in vain to try and make amends for this by charity organisations and unpaid magistracies. The cure must go deeper. It is no good trying to set straight the roof and chimneys, when the whole foundation is aslant. These good people are not boarded and lodged at Her Majesty's pleasure, but the Eternal Justice, unslumbering, causes them to build prisons (as I have said) for themselves—plagues them with ill-health and divers unseen evils—and will and must plague them, till such time as they shall abandon the impossible task they have set themselves, and return to the paths of reason.

The whole foundation is aslant—and *aslip*, as anyone may see who looks. In short, it is an age of transition. No mortal power could make durable a society founded on Usury—universal and boundless Usury. The very words scream at each other. The baron has passed away; and the landlord is passing. They each had their duties, and while they fulfilled them served their time well enough. The shareholder has no duties, and is an excrescence on the world, a public pest; and will remain so till the final landslip, when, the foundations having completely given way, he will crawl forth out of the ruins of his desirable mansion into the life and light of a new day.

Less oracular than this one may not be! As I

have said before, there is no conceivable condition of life in which the human soul may not find the materials of its surpassing deliverance from evil and mortality. And I for one would not, if I had the power, cramp human life into the exhibition of one universal routine. If anyone desires to be rich, if anyone desires to gradually shut himself off from the world, to build walls and fences, to live in a house where it is impossible to get a breath of fresh air without going through half a dozen doors, and to be the prisoner of his own servants; if he desires it so that when he walks down the street he cannot whistle or sing, or shout across the road to a friend, or sit upon a doorstep when tired, or take off his coat if it be hot, but must wear certain particular clothes in a certain particular way, and be on such pins and needles as to what he may or may not do, that he is right glad when he gets back again to his own prison walls; if he loves trusteeships and Egyptian bonds, and visits from the lawyer, and feels glad when he finds a letter from the High Court of Chancery on his breakfast-table, and experiences in attending to all these things that satisfaction which comes of all solid work; if he feels renovated and braced by lying in bed of a morning, and by eating feast dinners every day, and by carefully abstaining from any bodily labor; if dyspepsia and gout and biliousness are not otherwise than grateful to him; and if he can obtain all these things without doing grievous wrong to others, by all means let him have them.

Only for those who do not know what they desire I would lift up the red flag of warning. Only of that vast and ever vaster horde which to-day (chiefly, I cannot but think, in ignorance) rushes to Stocks, would I ask a moment's pause, and to look at the bare facts. If these words should come to the eye of such an one I would pray him to think for a moment— to glance at this great enthroned Wrong in its dungeon palace (not the less a wrong because the laws countenance and encourage it)—to listen for the cry of the homeless many, trodden under foot, a yearly sacrifice to it—to watch the self-inflicted sufferings of its worshipers, the ennui, the depression, the unlovely faces of ill-health—to observe the falsehood on which it is founded, and therefore the falsehood, the futility, the unbelief in God or Man which spring out of it—and to turn away, determined, as far as in him lies, to worship in that Dagon-house no longer.

SIMPLIFICATION OF LIFE.

"As I preferred some things to others, and especially valued my freedom, as I could fare hard and yet succeed well, I did not wish to spend my time in earning rich carpets or other fine furniture, or delicate cookery, or a house in the Grecian or the Gothic style just yet. If there are any to whom it is no interruption to acquire these things, and who know how to use them when acquired, I relinquish to them the pursuit."
—*Thoreau.*

CERTAINLY, if you do not want to be a vampire and a parasite upon others, the great question of practical life, and which everyone has to face, is how to carry it on with as little labor and effort as may be. No one wants to labor needlessly, and if you have to earn everything you spend, economy becomes a very personal question—not necessarily in the pinching sense, but merely as adaptation of means to the end. When I came some years ago to live with cottagers (earning say £50 to £60 a year) and share their life, I was surprised to find how little both in labor and expense their food cost them, who were doing far more work than I was, or indeed the generality of people among whom I had been living. This led me to see that the somewhat luxurious mode of living I had been accustomed to was a mere waste, as far as adaptation to any useful end was concerned; and afterwards I decided that it had been a positive hindrance, for when I became habituated to a more simple life and diet, I found that a marked improvement took place in my powers both of mind and body. At a later time when keeping house myself (still on the same scale, though with a little more latitude), and having, during a year or so, to buy *every* article of food, I found that the expense of feeding a family of four persons was under 8d. a head per diem, not including firing or labor of cooking. And now I am inclined to consider this needlessly large.

The difference, however, arising from having a small piece of garden is very great, and makes one feel how important it is that every cottage should have a plot of ground attached. A rood of land (quarter acre) is sufficient to grow all potatoes and other vegetables and some fruit for the year's use, say for a family of five. Half an acre would be an ample allowance. Such a piece of land may easily be cultivated by anyone in the odd hours of regular work, and the saving is naturally large from not having to go to the shop for everything of this nature that is needed. At the present time—October, 1885—when growing all fruit and vegetables, eggs also, for our own use, I find that our entire expenses for all other provisions (including flour, meat, milk, butter, groceries, etc.) amount to 5d. a head per day. The flour-bill (baking done at home) is about a 1d. per day each, and some portion of this —though I am not in a position at present to say exactly how much—is saved when we grow our own wheat. As a matter of practical interest I find that an acre of wheat in a fairly good year (say 10 "bags," or 180 stone) will provide a year's bread for a family of five. Anyone having a horse will of course find it economical to use it with the plough; but I am inclined to think that a cottager with a little more land than he would want for his garden, and with a little spare time, would find it worth while to *spade* up half an acre or so (he would get a rare crop in this way) and grow wheat on it. However, not having tried this plan myself, I will not do more than just to suggest it. A small hand-mill in the house serves with little labor to produce the whole-meal flour, but for white flour the corn must be sent to the miller.

While on this question of wheat I may remark that an impression seems to have got abroad that England is not a good wheat-producing country; but surely there is no ground for this. English grain is actually finer than the American grain, and the yield per acre on our farms is larger. As soon as ever we tried our own flour we found (really to our surprise) that the quality of bread was quite superior to what we had been accustomed to from the bought meal, and this in a district—the Derbyshire dales—by no means so well suited for corn growing as most parts of England. This purer taste of the bread may, however, have been partly due to the fact that millers and flour-dealers are in the habit of mixing different sorts and qualities of flour together (even if they do not adulterate with other substances), much as tea-blenders mix tea, and thus our bread of commerce, like everything else commercial, is sophisticated. The only serious drawback to English wheat is that in some rainy seasons the grain is not so dry as it should be—but millers, it must be remembered, have drying-floors. Undoubtedly the production of wheat in England is just now at a discount because of the extraordinary low-pricedness of the American wheat; but then it should be noted that the English farmer is frightfully burdened by our landlord system as well as by heavy rates and taxes. Whatever may be said about rent not entering into cost of production, and though the theory abstractly considered is a pretty one, yet in practice in England I believe it will be found to apply only very partially. The landlord is on the top of the farmer and has the advantage of him in every way. The latter is loth to leave the place on which he, and perhaps his ancestors before him, have lived so long, and to incur the disastrous expenses of a change; "hope springs eternal," and "though the seasons have been bad they may be better in the future;" then the available amount of land in the country is limited; there is always a large portion of the town population ready to try its hand at agriculture, if only as a hobby and in the face of probable loss; building speculations, favorableness of sites for ornamental estates, etc., re-act on agricultural rents; and though it is contended that all these things adjust themselves in *time*, yet it is just there that the difficulty arises. For during the time so required *the actual conditions of the problem change;* the prices, the cost of production, the situation of the "margin of cultivation" fluctuate, and their adjustment to rent in each particular case has to be re-discovered each year. The problem practically never is solved, but is deferred indefinitely; the landlord continues to reap the advantage of his strong and entrenched position, and the successive generations of burdened farmers, losing all their capital, and what is even more, all heart and courage, neglect their land, and widespread impoverishment, as now, ensues. This, being so, seems obviously a matter requiring immediate attention, for it must always be an object of first-class importance to a country to produce the staple articles of its own food; and if we find that our wheat-production is hampered even in a small degree by the obstruction of a privileged class, such obstruction ought to be removed as quickly as possible. Personally I am inclined to think, looking at all the details of the case and the indirect as well as direct influences, that this obstruction is not a small matter, and that though it does not by any means account for the entire difficulty which our farmers have in contending with American prices, it accounts for a large part of it, and is therefore a subject more serious and worthy of attention from our statesmen than for instance the opening up of new markets by petty foreign wars.

Another cause of the excessive import of foreign grain—especially American—is the action of the great railway companies, which to favor their carrying trade charge disproportionately low rates for their through traffic. In the United States, too, the great trunk lines, by their command of the wheat-producing districts, are enabled to exact ruinously low prices from the Western farmer, and so by throwing this low-priced wheat into England, are seriously damaging the agricultural interests on both sides of the water at the same time.

Again, as another curious instance of the artificial agencies at work, it may be mentioned that owing to the quantity of American wheat lately introduced into this country (and which is *drier* than the English grain), steel-roller machinery has been introduced into almost all our modern flour-mills. Now the steel-rollers *crush* the grain into flour instead of *grinding* it—but the English wheat is not dry and brittle enough to be crushed. The consequence is that when English wheat comes into the market, the millers do not care to buy it, and it suffers in price.

One more point. The American wheat, though really not so fine a grain as ours and not so nutritious, yields a *whiter* flour. And so the craze for whiteness of bread acts again in the same direction. I find the farmers here consider the English wheat quite as good for *eating*, if not better than the American, only—they say—the latter is more *eyeable*—*i.e.*, it looks better!

Thus we have the curious facts that England actually produces a larger yield of wheat per acre than America, and a finer and more nutritious grain; and yet that social conditions of one kind or another, the oppression of the agricultural interest by the carrying trade and by the landlord interest, and fashions and fancies in mills and flour, are all strongly handicapping our home-grown wheat, and even causing a prejudice that England is unfitted for its production.

To return to the question of domestic economy. Of course the current mode of life is so greatly wasteful, and we have come to consider so many things as necessaries—whether in food, furniture, clothing or what not—which really bring us back next to no profit or pleasure compared with the labor spent upon them, that it is really difficult to know where the balance of true economy would stand if, so to speak, left to itself. All we can do is to take the existing mode of life in its simpler forms, somewhat as above, and work from that as a basis. For though the cottager's way of living, say in our rural districts or in the neighborhood of our large towns, is certainly superior to that of the well-to-do, that does not argue that it is not capable of improvement.

About the largest account in most modern households is the butcher's. I find that our bill runs up to £10 a year, and this is less than in the Royal Household, where it reaches £9,472. If our princes and their attendants were to adopt a more frugal diet (say like that of the Caliph Omar, who rode from Medina to Jerusalem with a bag of dates and a bag of corn at his saddle-bow), they would probably be quite as cheerful and healthy as now, and there would be a great saving to the nation!

The causes of the craving for a meat diet seem to be similar to those of the craving for other stimulants. For though flesh is not generally considered a stimulant, a little attention will show that its action is of like nature. It very quickly produces a sense of wellbeing, liable to be followed by reaction and depression; and this action, though innocuous in its smaller degrees, becomes seriously harmful when flesh is made a staple article of diet. With regard to the healthfulness of stimulants generally, I am inclined to think that as long as they are merely used for *pleasure's* sake (sociality and good-fellowship) they are right enough, and in place; but as soon as ever they go so far as to become *necessities*, and the man learns to lean on them for support, or thinks that he cannot do without them, from that moment they are harmful and lowering to the system. The question of meat involves, of course, the additional question of our moral or sentimental relation to the animals. Probably the great craving for all these things goes with our present conditions of civilisation. The hurry, the overwork—or rather *feverish* work—of modern life; the bad air—as of women all along in the house, or men in a close workshop; the unnatural stimulations, in sexual affairs as in everything else; and above all the hypersensitiveness of our women, who, having abandoned outdoor life and labor, transmit a feebly nervous organism to the race:—all these things produce a craving for artificial supports. The man cannot walk and must have crutches; and the crutches in their turn enfeeble the limbs.

On the whole, and for habitual use, I do not know what can be pleasanter or more nourishing than the cereals (rice, wheat, etc.), milk, eggs, cheese, bread, butter, vegetables, and fruits of all kinds; and they seem to me to stand by one for hard work and endurance better than flesh. Excellent dishes can be compounded of these materials; though probably the less of cooking there is the better. As to the fearful and

SIMPLIFICATION OF LIFE. 103

wonderful recipes contained in the cookery books, the formula—*Serve up hot and throw out of the window*—might, with advantage, be appended to most of them. I am convinced there is a most abominable and idiotic waste of time in connection with this subject in all our well-to-do establishments. If the pleasure given bore any proportion to the expenditure of time and labor, there might be some sense in the matter, but it doesn't. Fancy a small household of five or six persons requiring a *cook*—*i.e.*, a person engaged all day long in preparing food for them. Is it not out of all reason? But the mistress of the house descends as it were from the skies, "orders dinner," and returns again to her celestial abode. Whether it was worth while that the scullery-maid should be sent scouring through the town, that she should return hot and tired, and quarrel with the cook—that saucepans should be soiled, much time consumed in peeling, and some money wasted—all in order that unseasonable shrimps should be made into indigestible sauce and served up with the fish, is a question which does not enter into her (the mistress's) head as she takes an infinitesimal portion of the said sauce upon her plate.

Once I had the honor of staying in a country house for a few days as a guest of one of the servants, and the view which I thus got of our social arrangements —from that side I suppose from which Moses saw the Almighty—was very curious and interesting.

The orthodox dinner, reduced even to its lowest terms, involves say meat, two vegetables, and a pudding—four dishes, all requiring cooking! The labor this represents per annum, and just for one meal a day,

is something fearful. And it is not a comfortable
meal; let alone the disagreeable smells involved in its
preparation—smells which necessitate sitting-rooms
being a long way from kitchens, and houses altogether
more extensive and cumbrous than they need be—it
is a meal having no centre of gravity; you cannot for
the life of you tell the proper proportion these dishes
bear to each other.

Would it not be better to have just one dish—(like
the family bowl seen in Highland cabins and elsewhere)
—one dish combining in itself all needful qualities of
nutrition and tastiness, with perhaps a few satellite
platters around for any adjuncts or off-sets that might
seem appropriate? This central dish (the only one
requiring immediate cookery), say some golden-orbed
substantial omelet, or vast vegetable pie, or savoury
and nutritious soup, or solid expanse of macaroni and
cheese, or steaming mountain of rice surrounded by
stewed fruit, or even plain bowl of fermenty, would
represent the sun or central fire of our system, while
round it in planetary order would circle such other
viands as would give the housewife a minimum of
trouble to provide—chunks of bread and cheese, figs,
raisins, oatmeal cakes, fresh fruit, or what not. Here
would no second relay of plates be necessary, and
victuals which could not face each other on the table
would not be forced into spiteful conflict within the
man. Even the knife and fork would almost disappear,
washing up would become an affair of a few minutes,
and the housewife's work before and after dinner be
reduced to a trifle compared with what it is now. For
it must be remembered that with this whole matter

hangs the question of women's work. Woman is a slave, and *must remain so* as long as ever our present domestic system is maintained. I say that our average mode of life, as conceived under the bourgeois ideal of society, cannot be kept up without perpetuating the slavery of woman. It is quite probable that in the mass she will resist the change; but it may have to come nevertheless.

As to the general question of eating, I am inclined to think that, as in other matters, though moderation is the best general rule, this has to be varied by an occasional orgy. For pleasure in the long run, health, economy of force, etc., a certain sparingness is to be recommended; but the orgy should not be omitted. Among other things it restores the moral tone, and prevents—a very important point—all danger of lapse into pharisaism! Probably if people nowadays had to slaughter for their own use the difficulty would be to get them to "kill the fatted calf." On my little farm we have fowls in plenty, but we cannot get one for dinner, simply because no member of the household is sufficiently goaded by hunger to be willing to perform the sacrifice: and so Peggy and Fluffy, though old, are respited from month to month, or taken to market—such is human inconsistency!—to be killed ultimately by someone else.

No doubt immense simplifications of our daily life are possible; but this does not seem to be a matter which has been much studied. Rather hitherto the tendency has been all the other way, and every additional ornament on the mantelpiece has been regarded as an acquisition, and not as a nuisance;

though one doesn't see any reason, in the nature of things, why it should be regarded as one more than the other. It cannot be too often remembered that every additional object in a house requires additional dusting, cleaning, repairing ; and lucky are you if its requirements stop there. When you abandon a wholesome tile or stone floor for a Turkey carpet, you are setting out on a voyage of which you cannot see the end. The Turkey carpet makes the old furniture look uncomfortable, and calls for stuffed couches and armchairs; the couches and armchairs demand a walnut-wood table; the walnutwood table requires polishing, and the polish bottles require shelves; the couches and armchairs have casters and springs, which give way and want mending ; they have damask seats, which fade and must be covered ; the chintz covers require washing, and when washed they call for antimacassars to keep them clean. The antimacassars require wool, and the wool requires knitting-needles, and the knitting-needles require a box, the box demands a side-table to stand on, and the side-table involves more covers and castors—and so we go on. Meanwhile the carpet wears out and has to be supplemented by bits of drugget, or eked out with oilcloth, and, beside the daily toil required to keep this mass of rubbish in order, we have every week or month, instead of the pleasant cleaning-day of old times, a terrible domestic convulsion and *bouleversement* of the household.

It is said by those who have travelled in Arabia that the reason why there are so many religious enthusiasts in that country, is that in the extreme

SIMPLIFICATION OF LIFE. 107

simplicity of the life and uniformity of the landscape there *heaven*—in the form of the intense blue sky—seems close upon one. One may almost see God. But we moderns guard ourselves effectually against this danger. For beside the smoke pall which covers our towns, we raise in each household such a dust of trivialities that our attention is fairly absorbed, and if this screen subsides for a moment we are sure to have the daily paper held up before our eyes—so that if a chariot of fire were sent to fetch us, ten to one we should not see it.

However, if this multiplying of the complexity of life is really grateful to some people, one cannot quarrel with them for pursuing it; and to many it appears to be so. When a sewing-machine is introduced into a household the simple-minded husband thinks that, as it works ten times as quick as the hand, there will now be only a tenth part of the time spent by his wife and daughter in sewing that there was before. But he is ignorant of human nature. To his surprise he finds that there is *no* difference in the time. The difference is in the plaits and flounces—they put ten times as many on their dresses.

Thus we see how little *external* reforms avail. If the *desire* for simplicity is not really present, no labor-saving appliances will make life simpler.

Talking about floors, it seems a good plan in upper chambers, and rooms where floors are boarded, to stain and varnish them. This is not expensive, but it takes a little time—two or three days altogether for the different washes to dry; first the stain, then a wash of size, *i.e.*, diluted glue, and then the oak or

other varnish. The advantage of varnished floors is
that they do not require scrubbing, which is a very
laborious process, but only to be rubbed over with a
wet cloth. One or two rugs, or bits of carpet, are all
that is needed for a covering, and these can be easily
taken up and shaken, and the room swept at the weekly
cleaning. A carpet over the whole floor not only
smells badly, and makes the air of the room perman-
ently stuffy, but, being difficult to remove, it remains
down for months at a time, and harbors all sorts of
dirt. Varnished floors, however, will not stand heavy
work, as in a living-room or kitchen where thick boots
are in and out all day; and here stone or tile floors,
with cocoa-nut or other matting if a covering is
wanted, always seems to me the most appropriate.

The rest of the furniture takes its cue very much
from the treatment of the floor. As a rule all
curtains, hangings, cloths, and covers, which are not
absolutely necessary, should be dispensed with. They
all create dust and stuffiness, and all entail trouble
and recurring expense, and they all tempt the house-
keeper to keep out the air and sunlight—two things
of the last and most vital importance. I like a room
which looks its best when the sun streams into it
through wide open windows and doors. If the fur-
nishing of it cannot stand this test—if it looks
uncomfortable under the operation—you may be sure
there is something unwholesome about it. As to the
question of elegance or adornment, that may safely be
left to itself. The studied effort to make interiors
elegant has only ended—in what we see. After all, if
things are *in their place* they will always look well.

What, by common consent, is more graceful than a
ship—the sails, the spars, the rigging, the lines of the
hull? Yet go on board and you will scarcely find one
thing placed there for the purpose of adornment. An
imperious necessity rules everything; this rope *could*
have no other place than it has, nor could be less
thick or thicker than it is; and it is, in fact, this
necessity which makes the ship beautiful. Everything
in it *has relation*—has relation to the winds and
waves, or to something else on board, and is there for
purposes beyond its own existence. Or again, after
you have been the round of æsthetically-furnished
mansions, and seen all that taste and wealth can do
in this direction, does it not happen to you at last to
turn by chance into some old-fashioned cottage by
the wayside, and find that, for pure grace and beauty,
this interior, without the least effort or intention whatever,
has beaten all the rest hollow? Yet, with the
exception perhaps of a few plants in the window,
everything here is for use. The eye rests on nothing
but what suggests a train of thought. Here is the
axe hanging, there the gun; here over the dresser a
row of plates, there the kettle boiling on the fire; and
there, behind the door, the straw hat which the rosy-cheeked
girl puts on when she runs out to look to the
fowls. Everything is alive, and transparent too with
cleanly human life. But your modern drawing-room
is dead—a stupor comes over the mind as it gazes at
the aimless armchairs, and the room seems full of
lumber. You cannot *make* your room beautiful by
buying an expensive vase and putting it on the
mantel-shelf; but if you live an honest life in it, it

will *grow* beautiful in proportion as it comes to answer to the wants of such a life.

The treatment of walls is a somewhat vexed question. Some people prefer paper, while others prefer a color-wash or paint. On the whole there always seems to me something incongruous and even trivial in the idea of *papering* stone and plaster. Color-washes are clean and sweet; they are made of whitening with a little size (or flour and water) mixed to prevent rubbing off, and coloring matter according to choice. They are of course quite inexpensive, and can be renewed every two or three years. Paint has the advantage of being very durable and of being washable, but it has the drawback of being more laborious and costly in operation, and of course renders a room uninhabitable for a week or two till it is thoroughly dry. In fact care should be taken with regard to this last point. On the whole I think papering is the least trouble, color-washing the least expensive in materials, and paint perhaps the most satisfactory in the long run. If, however, a room is really well plastered to begin with (which does not often happen nowadays), one may very well dispense with all three methods, and that is perhaps after all the most obvious thing to do.

With regard to clothing, as with furniture and the other things, it can be much simplified if one only desires it so. Probably, however, most people do not desire it, and of course they are right in keeping to the complications. Who knows but what there is some influence at work for some ulterior purpose which we do not guess, causing us to artificialise our lives to the extraordinary extent we do in modern times? Our ancestors wore woad, and it does not at first sight seem obvious why we should not do the same. Without, however, entering into the woad question, we may consider some ways in which clothing may be simplified without departing far from the existing standard. It seems to be generally admitted now that wool is the most suitable material as a rule. I find that a good woollen coat, such as ordinarily worn, feels warmer when *unlined* than it does when a layer of silk or cotton is interposed between the woollen surface and the body. It is also lighter; thus in both ways the simplification is a gain. Another advantage is that it washes easier and better, and is at all times cleaner. No one who has had the curiosity once to unpick the lining of a tailor-made coat that has been in wear a little time, will, I think, ever wish to have coats made on the same principle again. The rubbish he will find inside, the frettings and frayings of the cloth collected in little dirt-heaps up and down, the paddings of cotton wool, the odd lots of miscellaneous stuff used as backings, the quantity of canvas stiffening, the tags and paraphernalia connected with the pockets, bits of buckram inserted here and there to make the coat "sit" well— all these things will be a warning to him. What would be shamed by exposure to the light is all covered up by a sham decorous lining, and if the mess looks unwholesome and suggestive of disease in a comparatively new coat made by a well-to-do tailor, what must it be in the case of a coat made up by a cheap and nasty dealer, or one that has been unwashed (and how can one wash such a thing?) for years?

Now if all these tags are done away with, and a coat is made up of *good* cloth without any lining whatever or any stiffening (except a patch here and there where the buttons are sewn on), and with pockets simply made by the addition of another patch of cloth—patch-pockets as they are called—the relief and the sense of added comfort, warmth, lightness, cleanliness, are really delightful. The truth is that one might almost as well be in one's coffin as in the stiff layers upon layers of buckram-like clothing commonly worn nowadays. No genial influence from air or sky can pierce this dead hide, no effluence from within escape. A man's clothing we will say generally consists round his trunk of undervest, shirt, waistcoat and coat, to which must sometimes be added an overcoat—each of the three last-mentioned garments consists, at any rate over the front of the body, of *three* thicknesses—cloth, canvas-stiffening, and lining—in all eleven layers. Eleven layers between him and God! No wonder the Arabian has the advantage over us. Who could be inspired under all this weight of tailordom?

And certainly, nowadays, many folk visibly *are* in their coffins. Only the head and the hands out, all the rest of the body clearly sickly with want of light and air, atrophied, stiff in the joints, strait-waistcoated, and partially mummied. Sometimes it seems to me that is the reason why, in our modern times, the curious intellect is so abnormally developed, the brain and the tongue waggle so, because these organs alone have a chance, the rest are shut out from heaven's light and air: the poor human heart grown feeble and weary in its isolation and imprisonment, the sexual parts degenerated and ashamed of themselves, the liver diseased, and the lungs straitened down to mere sighs and conventional disconsolate sounds beneath their cerements.

But a good woollen shirt and coat, and pants of similar material, are really all a man needs for ordinary wear in our climate—three garments, all simply made, easily washable, and often washed. In quite cold weather a waistcoat can be added, which should also be unlined, and with the back made out of cloth the same as the front. Thus, even when a greatcoat is worn, the maximum will be only four thicknesses over the body instead of eleven, while the normal covering will be two layers instead of eight. The warmth will be just as great as before, but the suffocation and mummydom will be less; we shall be nearer the sources of life, and may possibly even hear spoken to *us* the words: "Lazarus, come forth!"

As to the feet, which have been condemned to their leathern coffins so long that we are almost ashamed to look at them, there is still surely a resurrection possible for them. There seems to be no reason except mere habit why, for a large part of the year at least, we should not go barefoot, as the Irish do, or at least with sandals. [Democracy, which redeems the lowest and most despised of the people, must redeem also the most menial and despised members and organs of the body.] Even now, effeminated as our feet are, it takes but little practice to accustom them to country roads; in our towns with their excellent pavements the custom might in summer time be adopted at once. And who does not know the pleasure of grasping the ground—the bare earth—with his bare feet? If it be objected that it is really impossible to imagine our modern life carried on on such principles—the brokers on the London Stock-Exchange hurrying around, or the visitor appearing at a fashionable afternoon tea, in bare feet (!)—this is not a serious argument; because if the two things are really incompatible, it is quite possible that in the long run the Stock-Exchange and afternoon-tea business may turn out to be the less important of the two—less grounded in the ultimate necessity of things than the freedom and emancipation of a single member of the human body; and so the little toe, like the proverbial worm, though nearly crushed, may at last turn and revenge itself on a civilisation whose oppression it has too long endured.

But, as we are talking about economy, what a saving of labor and expense would be effected by dispensing, if only for six months out of the year, with shoes and stockings! The labor involved in merely *darning* the latter is really a serious item in household life. Though scoffed at by the male part of the community, as beneath their notice—this labor is only another of the links in the chain which binds the women-folk down. Again, who does not know the time which is spent, in any self-supporting household, in patching and mending the numerous garments worn, putting in fresh linings and renewing pockets?—time which might be largely saved if the number of garments was much reduced, and their construction altogether simplified from the beginning. Thus, all through for men, and similarly for women, a simplification of dress might be adopted—even without departing far from present modes—which would involve far less initial expense, and far less labor of maintenance than the present plan. And if these things seem trivial to some well-bred person, who is in the habit of saying, like the Centurion in the Bible, to his servant:—"Do this, and he doeth it"—we must remember, as was said at the outset, that in any honest household, faithfully providing for its own wants, such matters *have* to be faced. The husband *has* out of his labor to provide the initial expense, the wife has to do the most part of the work of repair and renewal, and to such people the affair is not trivial at all. Rather one might say that if educated and wealthy people would set the example of solving such questions to the utmost in their own persons, they would do more to lighten the burden of life for the mass of the people than they can expect to do by casually plunging their hands into their pockets in aid of some Charity.

There are many other ways in which the details and labor of daily life may be advantageously reduced, which will occur to anyone who turns practical attention to the matter. For myself I confess to a great pleasure in witnessing the Economies of Life—and how seemingly nothing need be wasted; how the very stones that offend the spade in the garden become invaluable when footpaths have to be laid out or drains to be made. Hats that are past wear get cut up into strips for nailing creepers to the wall; the upper leathers of old shoes are useful for the same purpose. The under garment that is too far gone for mending is used for patching another less decrepit of its kind, then it is torn up into strips for bandages, or what not; and when it has served its time thus it descends to floor-washing, and is scrubbed out of life—useful to the end. When my coat has worn itself into an affectionate intimacy with my body, when it has served for Sunday best, and for weekdays, and got weather-stained out in the fields with sun and rain—then, faithful, it does not part from me, but getting itself cut up into shreds and patches descends to form a hearthrug for my feet. After that, when worn through, it goes into the kennel and keeps my dog warm, and so after lapse of years, retiring to the manure-heaps and passing out onto the land, returns to me in the form of potatoes for my dinner; or, being pastured by my sheep, reappears upon their backs as the material of new clothing. Thus it remains a friend to all time, grateful to me for not having despised and thrown it away when it first got behind the fashions. And seeing we have been faithful to each other, my coat and I, for one round or life-period, I do not see why we should not renew our intimacy—in other metamorphoses—or why we should ever quite lose touch of each other through the aeons.

With regard to the sum-total of labor required for the maintenance of a household according to modern notions, I find on my little farm of seven acres (which is by no means conducted on model principles, but in a very ordinary way) that the figures for last financial year (September '84-'85) run as follows:—

Number of persons, rather over four on the average; household expenses (including provisions, but not clothing or personal expenses), £38; farm expenses, *i.e.*, seeds, tools, manure, etc., £15; taxes, £6; close upon £60 in all. I consider that the farm and market garden could easily be worked by a man and his family, say having a son of fifteen to help him, with just occasional outside help. And the question then would be for them to sell stuff sufficient to cover the above outlay and leave a margin for pocket-money and *rent* (payable, we should hope, to the nation, and not to any individual landlord). This they ought to do, and probably would do without difficulty in times of average prices. What exact margin might be expected, or what exact extent of land would yield the best results, are questions which I should find it difficult to answer; all such points depend so very much on considerations of soil, locality, kinds of crop grown, whether ordinary or highly specialised, the state of the markets, etc., that it seems rash and indeed impossible to generalise on them. Personally I feel so very strongly that the present conditions of commercial production are rapidly passing away, that I don't think it very much matters whether the peasant occupier (or any other worker or industrial adventurer) is proved to be a commercial success or a commercial failure just now. When the new conditions of society enable the worker to receive something like an equivalent of the value he produces[1], it is evident that the question of success

[1] Mr. Mulhall (*Dictionary of Statistics*) gives, for 1883, our national produce of wealth at value £1,265,000,000; number of families of producers, 4,629,000. Dividing, we find that £273 a year is the average value produced by each family.

or failure will be a very different one from what it is to-day.

What I feel more interested to show is the actual expenses—as in the figures given above—of carrying on a simple, but unstinted, household life. For though some would consider these figures absurdly small, and others needlessly large, yet on the whole they are probably not far from the average experience on the subject; and at any rate I give them because I can vouch for their accuracy. Not long ago a gentleman told me that he was anxious to adopt a very simple mode of life, and to take a cottage with a plot of land to it, for himself and family, but was waiting till he had saved money enough—£15,000 *was the sum he mentioned*—for the venture. I thought it was a pity he should wait so long for so expensive a simplicity!

In the more or less socialistic state of society towards which we seem to be trending, the normal condition would probably be for a man to have a cottage and sufficient land—say half an acre—to grow a good deal of food for his own use, while daily labor at a really adequate rate of wages would be secured to him outside in workshop, design-room, school, warehouse, or wherever it might be. And this always seems to me, if properly managed, the most satisfactory mode of life for the average man. It avoids the uncertainties and anxieties of running a concern of one's own. There is no reason why the wage-work should not be done under pleasant and wholesome conditions, the hours need not be long, and there would be a home and land of one's own on which to expend superfluous energy. Thus, if we take the household expenses at

£40, including purchase of a few tools, etc., for the garden, and rent (payable to the State, and therefore no taxes) at £10, we see that a family earning £100 a year would have ample margin for clothing, pocket-money, and even travelling within reasonable limits—would be, in fact, quite well off. But even under the present wasteful conditions of society, statistics show, as in the note on last page, that the value created by each family of producers is over £270 a year. Allowing something, then, for the expenses of distribution, organisation, etc., and even allowing *nothing* for the improved productiveness of labor under a better system—we still see that the normal wage per annum may be placed at something like £250 per family. This would be, of course, under the supposition that the hours of labor remained the same as they are now. In this respect, however, under any reasonable condition of society, a man would be at liberty to exercise some choice. If he wished to live *very* luxuriously, or had extraordinary expenses to meet, he could continue working his nine or ten hours as now; if, however, his domestic wants were only about the ordinary range, they would easily be covered by the sum (£100) we have mentioned, and then obviously four hours a day would be sufficient; while if single, and of simple habits, he (or she) could do with less.

In the above sketch my object has been not so much to put forward any theory of the conduct of daily life, or to maintain that one method of living is of itself superior to another, as to try and come at the *facts* connected with the subject. In the long run every household *has* to support itself; the benefits and accommodations it receives from society have to be covered by the labor it expends for society. This cannot be got over. The present effort of a large number of people to live on interest and dividends, and so in a variety of ways on the labor of *others*, is simply an effort to make water run up hill: it cannot last very long. The balance, then, between the labor that you consume and the labor that you expend may be struck in many different ways, but it has to be struck; and I have been interested to bring together some materials for an easy solution of the problem.

DOES IT PAY?

> "Who has been wise receives interest."
> —*Walt Whitman.*

HAVING lately embarked in an agricultural enterprise on a small scale, I confess I was somewhat disconcerted, if not actually annoyed, by the persistency with which—from the very outset and when I had been only two or three months at work—I was met by the question at the head of this paper. Not only sisters, cousins and aunts, but relatives much more remote, and mere acquaintances, at the very first suggestion that I was engaged in trade, always plumped out with the query, Does it pay? And this struck me the more because, though I knew the point was important, I had in the innocence of my heart fancied that there might be other considerations of at least comparable weight. But I soon found out my mistake; for none of my well-to-do friends asked whether the work I was doing was wanted, or whether it would be useful to the community, or a means of healthy life to those engaged in it, or whether it was *honest* and of a kind that could be carried on without interior defilement; or even (except one or two) whether I liked it, but always: Does it pay? I say my well-to-do friends, because I couldn't help remarking that while the workers generally asked me such questions as whether the soil was good, or adapted to the purpose, the crops fine, the water abundant, etc., it was always the rich who asked the distinctively commercial question—a professional question, as it appeared to me, and which marked them as a class, and their modes of thought. Not that I have any quarrel with them for asking it, because the question is undoubtedly in some sense a very important one, and one which has to be asked; rather I ought to feel grateful and indebted, because it forced me to think about a matter that I had not perhaps fully considered before.

What then did it mean? What was the exact sense of the expression, Does it pay? as here used? On inquiring, I found it came to this: "When you have subtracted from your gross receipts all expenses for wages of labor, materials, etc., is there a balance equivalent to four or five per cent. on your outlay of capital? If yes, it pays; if no, it doesn't." Clearly if the thing came up to this standard or surpassed it, it was worthy of attention; if it didn't, it would be dismissed as unimportant, and soon be dropped and abandoned. This was clear and definite, and at first I felt greatly relieved to have arrived at so solid a conclusion. But after a time, and carrying on the enterprise farther, I am sorry to say that my ideas (for they have a great tendency that way) again began to get misty, and I could not feel sure that I had arrived at any certain principle of action.

My difficulty was that I began to feel that even supposing the concern only brought me in *one* per

cent. on my capital, it was quite as likely as not that
I should still stick to it. For I thought that if I was
happy in the life, and those working with me were
well content too, and if there were children growing
up on the place under tolerably decent and healthy
conditions, and if we were cultivating genuine and
useful products—cabbages and apples or what not—
that it might really pay me better to get one per
cent. for that result, even if it involved living quite
simply and inexpensively, than ten per cent. with
jangling and wrangling, over-worked and sad faces
round me, and dirty and deceptive stuff produced;
and that if I could afford it, I might even think it
worth while to *pay* to keep the first stage going,
rather than *be* paid for the second.

I knew it was very foolish of me to think so, and
bad political economy, and I was heartily ashamed
of myself, but still I couldn't help it. I knew the
P. E.'s would say that if I disregarded the interest on
my capital I should only be disturbing natural adjustments, that my five per cent. was an index of
what was wanted, a kind of providential arrangement
harmonising my interest (literally) with that of the
mass of mankind, and that if I was getting only one
per cent. while others were sending in the same stuff
from France and getting ten per cent., it was clear
that I was wasting labor by trying to do here what
could be done so much more profitably somewhere
else, and that I ought to give way. This was what I
knew they would say; but then from my own little
experience I readily saw that the ten per cent. profit
in France or elsewhere might mean no superior ad-

vantage of labor in that part, but merely superior grinding and oppression of the laborer by the employer, superior disadvantage of the laborer, in fact; and that if I gave way in its favor, I should only be encouraging the extortion system. I should be playing into the hands of some nefarious taskmaster in another part of the industrial world, and by increasing his profits should perhaps encourage others, still more unscrupulous, to undersell him, which of course they would do by further exactions from the worker; and so on and on. I saw too that if I abandoned my enterprise, I should have to discharge my workpeople, with great chance of their getting no fresh employment, and to them I had foolishly become quite attached; which was another serious trouble, but I could not help it.

And so in all this confusion of mind, and feeling quite certain that I could not understand all the complexities of the science of Political Economy myself, and having a lurking suspicion that even the most able professors were in the dark about some points, I began to wonder if the most sensible and obvious thing to do were not just to try and keep at least one little spot of earth clean: actually to try and produce clean and unadulterated food, to encourage honest work, to cultivate decent and healthful conditions for the workers, and useful products for the public, and to maintain this state of affairs as long as I was able, taking my chance of the pecuniary result to myself. It would not be much, but it would be something, just a little glimmer, as it were, in the darkness; but if others did the same, the illumination would increase, and after a time perhaps we should all be able to see our way better.

I knew that this method of procedure would not be "scientific"—that it would be beginning at the wrong end for that; but, then as I have said, I felt in despair about my ever being clever enough really to understand the science—and as to half-knowledge, that might be more misleading than none. It was like the advice in the Bible, "Seek ye first the kingdom of God, and his righteousness, and all these things shall be added unto you," obviously irrational and absurd, and any argument would expose the fallacy of it, and yet I felt inclined to adopt it.

For when, on the other hand, I tried to make a start along the ordinary lines, I found myself from the outset in a hopeless bog! I could not, for the life of me, tell *how much* I ought to take as interest, and how much I ought to give in wages—the increase of the former evidently depending on the smallness of the latter. If I adopted just the current rate of wages, there was nothing in that, for I knew that they represented a mere balance of extortion on the one hand and despair on the other, and how could I take that as my principle of action? If I gave more than the current rate I should very likely get no interest at all, and so be consigned to perdition by all my well-to-do friends, including the Professors o. Political Economy; while, if I gave less, I should certainly go to hell in my own eyes. And though I pondered over this dilemma, or rather trilemma, till I was sick of it, I never could see my way out of it.

And then I reflected that even if I was lucky

enough to pitch on some principle of wage-payment
which would leave a nice little balance of interest,
it was quite doubtful whether I should feel any right
to appropriate such balance to my own use. That
also was a great trouble, for I could not help seeing that after taking my proportional payment for
my labors in the concern, and some small remuneration for my care of superintendence, if I then appropriated a considerable interest on the capital laid
out, I should, without any extra work, be much better off than my coadjutors. And though the P. E.'s
assured me this was all right, and kind of providential, I had serious qualms which, do what I
would, I could not shake off. I felt keenly that what
I should then be taking would only be so much subtracted from the wages of these others, and that the
knowledge of this would disturb the straightforward
relation between us, and I should no longer be able
to look them in the face.

I could not help seeing too that it was by means of
this *general system of the appropriation of balances*
that a very curious phenomenon was kept up---an
enormous class, to wit, living in idleness and luxury,
they and their children and their children's children,
till they became quite incapable of doing anything
for themselves or even of thinking rightly about
most things, tormented with incurable *ennui* and
general imbecility and futility; all art and literature, which were the appendage of this class, being
affected by a kind of St. Vitus' dance; and the whole
thing breaking out finally for want of any other occupation into a cuff and collar cult, called respectability,

And then I began to see more clearly the meaning of the question (asked by this class), *Does it pay?*—i.e., Can we continue drawing from the people nourishment enough to keep our St. Vitus' dance going? I thought I saw a vision of poor convulsed creatures, decked out in strange finery, in continual antic dance, peering in each other's faces with eager questioning as to whether the state of profits would allow the same doleful occupation to go on for ever. And all the more eager I saw them on account of the dim wandering consciousness they had that the whole thing was not natural and right, and the presentiment that it could not last very long. And then I saw a vision of the new society in which the appropriation of balances was not the whole object of life; but things were produced primarily for the use and benefit of those who should consume them. It was actually thought that it *paid better* to work on that principle; and strangely enough, the kingdom of heaven was at the centre of that society—and the "other things" were added unto it. But there was no respectability there, for the balances that could be privately appropriated were not large enough even to buy starch with, and a great many people actually went without collars.

And so I saw that the eager question (in the particular sense in which it had been asked me) was in fact a symptom of the decay of the old society—a kind of dying grin and death-rattle of respectability—and that a new order, a new life, was already preparing beneath the old, in which there would be no need for it to be asked; or if asked, then in which it should be asked in a new sense.

TRADE.

"He likewise engaged in a pursuit disgraceful even in a private individual—buying great quantities of goods and selling them again to advantage."—*Suetonius* concerning Vespasian.

I SUPPOSE the peculiar character of our commercial age—its excellencies and its defects—can be as well studied in the market as anywhere. The first time I stood behind my own goods, and spread out peas and potatoes, roses and raspberries of my own growing to the eye of the customer, I felt that I was passing behind a veil, many things were becoming clear! I had often been in the market as a buyer, and had, I am sorry to say, been accustomed to look upon a tradesman as the personification of artful wickedness —one who combined with his fellows to defraud the public and to take advantage of its innocence. But now I had passed myself into that inner circle, and with what a different eye did I regard the situation! It seemed to me now that it was the public which was at fault. I seemed to see at a glance the original sinfulness of its disposition. How out of its naughty old heart it suspected you always and always of putting the bad stuff at the bottom of the basket; how it would beat you down shamelessly, if it could, to prices below the zero of any possible remuneration to the grower; how it would handle fruit and flowers till all the delicate bloom was gone, and then pass by with a scoff; and how, instead of desiring to do to others as it would be done by, its one guiding fear, overruling all lesser sentiments of honesty and humanity, was lest it should be *done* by others as it would desire to *do* them. Hitherto I had looked upon cheap goods as a blessing, but now I saw, or seemed to see, that they meant general ruin. For cheap goods meant low wages, scarcity of money; meant hungry faces going by, and hands fingering halfpence long and anxiously before parting with them; meant slow sales and poor returns to the trader. While scarcity and high prices seemed no longer the unmixed evil I had supposed, for likely as not they were the indication of a brisk demand, full pockets, and general prosperity.

Thus my change of position, from the front to the back of a stall, wrought at once a considerable alteration in my views of some social matters. I took a new view of the world. My axiom was changed, and consequently a lot of theorems, which I thought were well established, fell to pieces, and became sadly invalid. I found the inner circle of the market a vantage ground, too, for the study of human nature. Here the buyers are the performers. They occupy the arena, and are exposed to a considerable criticism from behind the stalls. The seller, on the other hand, is comparatively unobserved. The buyer eyes the strawberries, old bird though he be he cannot entirely hide the gleam of his satisfaction at their appearance.

"How much?" he asks carelessly. "Five shillings a peck," is your equally careless reply. You know the fruit is first rate. You know also that he knows it; and he probably knows that you know that he knows it. "Eh, what are you talking about?" is his answer, and in assumed disgust he goes off down the market. Presently you see him coming back again; he has been all round; but as he goes by, crafty, he scarce glances at the coveted stuff. Not till he has got to a safe distance, and to a spot where he thinks he may stand unobserved does he turn again and measure it over with his eye. Now then you are satisfied; you know that you are safe about those strawberries, and you may give your attention to the sale of other things. You know also (what is very important) that there is no better fruit of the same kind and at the same price in the market. Great is your triumph when, after some delay, your customer returns (as he infallibly will do) and you are able to tell him that the produce in question is all sold, or that the *price has risen!*

On the whole, though the maxims of business are not too lofty, the thorough business people are the most satisfactory to deal with. They waste no time in whatever higgling is necessary, they know a little of both sides of the question, and are inclined to treat you as a reasonable creature, and are prompt and methodical. This carefully-dressed, somewhat stout matron with curls looks a little old-fashioned, but she has a shrewd eye and a kindly heart; she keeps a shop, and knows pretty well how prices stand both for buyer and seller; is pleasant to deal with, and not disinclined to put her customer on a friendly and permanent footing. Here comes a man who considers himself quite the boss of the market—brisk and business-like, with extensive watch chain, and elegant flower in his buttonhole; he is a large dealer, and acts as if he were doing you the honor to be your customer. Nevertheless one can get on with him; but this abominable Irishwoman, who always turns up talking nineteen to the dozen, and wanting to beg everything at shameless prices, and then when the bargain is concluded asking for this to be thrown in and that to be thrown in, is really more than I can bear. Then there is an unpleasant-looking ferret-eyed man who always suspects me of having put the best potatoes at the top; I do not like him, and feel no satisfaction in selling anything to him. But this little man in carefully-brushed great-coat and tall hat is really a pleasure to deal with. He is a retail customer, and is quite a Pickwickian study, has an immense red nose, which must occupy nearly all his field of view, yet of drinking I am sure he is blameless, so affable and scrupulous is he; and when he buys a peck of peas I feel certain he will take them home and shell them sitting by his wife's side. There is the working wife too, who wants a nice cauliflower for the Sunday dinner, but ultimately decides on a cabbage on account of the price; and the young man who wants a buttonhole for his girl. He chooses the most lovely of the rosebuds, but pauses when he hears what he has to pay (for the season is advanced)—he retires for a moment, and then comes forward like a man and secures his prize.

Those who know something about the labor of production—either in the trade in question or in some other trade—are often most reasonable to deal with. They can sympathise to some extent with you. I find that the "lady" or "gentleman" is often inclined to beat one down or refuse a rational price out of mere ignorance; not knowing what they ought to give, they assume that whatever you ask must be an imposition. And of course, on the other hand, they often *are* imposed upon by the unscrupulous. I confess that I have been inclined to take this latter part myself. There is a widespread impression among the "people" that the wealthy class are lawful prey. Perhaps they are—it might be difficult to decide one way or the other—but anyhow the gap or the want of sympathetic relation between the two parties makes their dealings with one another unsatisfactory.

With regard to the higgling of the prices, and the law of supply and demand, it is interesting to see how rapidly you *feel* from your own particular stand the general state of the market, how organically you seem to form a part of it. You drive over the hills by sunrise, plunging down through the clear light and by the dewy hedgerows into the still quiet streets of the great city; you find yourself in a bustling, noisy market, you open out your goods, take a cursory glance at the quantity of stuff in of various kinds, and mentally fix on the probable prices. The stream of customers flows by. "How much?" "How much?" "How much?" Different as are the characters of the individuals comprising the crowd, various as are their little dodges and artifices, the total effect is soon averaged. As you reply to each, expressions of disgust or satisfaction involuntarily pass over their faces, and in a few minutes you know quite certainly how you stand—your little gland which is washed by the general circulation soon gets congested with traffic or left high and dry—and your relation to the rest of the market is established.

I should be inclined to think that, unless it be the petroleum market, there is no market which fluctuates so rapidly as the vegetable and fruit market. Frosts spoil tons of cauliflowers, rain ruins acres of strawberries; a few fine days in spring will cause parsley to fall from three shillings a pound to as many pence.

From week to week in some articles it is impossible to tell what the price will be. You bring in a load of fine celery roots and the market is glutted with celery, there are tons and tons in, and it is as good as given away to the street-hawkers; another day it is just as scarce—everyone has held back—and poor stuff fetches a good price. Even from hour to hour the variations are remarkable; some things will run out and run up, other things will remain abundant to the very close of the market, and have to be sold at last for a mere song. Quite a class of small traders and hawkers lie in wait for this last casualty, and make their living by buying what else would be shot up on the manure heap. Still, though competition thus holds sway and can, so to speak, be felt in operation, it is difficult to reduce the law of supply and demand to anything like an absolute generalisation, or to make it practically applicable except in the roughest way. Custom, which is a force antagonistic to competition, and which has at one time undoubtedly been the main determinant of prices—which is certainly one of the

strongest forces of human nature, and which will have
to be reckoned with in any forecast of the future
adjustments of commerce—custom acts strongly to-
day in the markets, even in the very teeth of the
fierce competition that exists. Customary prices
modify competition prices; for very shame large
numbers of people will not buy and will not sell at
rates which they consider abnormal; a latent sense
of honor withholds them; the tendency of buyers
and sellers to establish permanent and friendly dealings with each other, a tendency which I am inclined
to think lies at the base of all exchange and which
has created, I suppose, the word "customer," is still
quite strongly traceable, the effort of the human to
assert itself as against the merely mechanical being
yet not quite extinct. Then there are nameless pre-
ferences—as of individuals for particular varieties of
goods—or of classes of buyers for particular classes of
sellers; nameless habits, traditions, predilections or
prejudices, and this in every trade, anomalies which
competition ought to level down, but somehow it does
not. Undoubtedly the *tendency* to a mechanical level
may be said to exist, but that the level or anything
like a level is ever reached is quite a different thing.
It is like a basin of water being carried about in the
hand; the water should go horizontal; but the disturb-
ances arising from the human side effectually prevent
this being realised. Thus competition when one becomes practically acquainted with it, when one comes
to *feel* its operation, appears somewhat as a force
acting on the human—acting, I would almost say, to
degrade or warp the human within one. It does not

appear as an isolated and self-sufficient law of exchange, but just as one factor in the problem, a factor which, if it had everything its own way, would speedily reduce commerce to a mere mechanical function devoid of all humanity. This, however, is a result which is impossible, because no function of human nature can be separated from humanity and made purely mechanical without *ipso facto* withering away and dying. And thus we have the alternative that commerce must either go on in its present direction and perish, or live by returning to human relationship as its basis.

"I have tried trade," says Thoreau, " but I found it would take ten years to get under-way in that, and that then I should probably be on my way to the devil." And again he says, " Trade curses everything it handles." I myself have never met anyone who seriously maintained that success in trade was in the long run compatible with honesty. These charges, however, may not be so damnatory as they appear, for after all perhaps it does not matter so much whether trade *can* be carried on honestly or not, as whether you *try* to carry it on honestly. The use of trade, as perhaps of every other pursuit, is mainly to test your probity; and I should say that for that purpose it is excellently adapted. The strains it puts upon you are severe. If, however, folks generally tried to carry on trade honestly, very probably a new form of exchange would soon develop itself which would allow of honesty being realised.

I do not think that the difficulty about trade lies chiefly in the market, but rather in its influence, indirectly, on production. The market, on the whole, with all its chicanery, its worship of 'cuteness, its besting and bluffing, is an intensely human institution; the very fact that you are forced into contact with such a number of your fellow-creatures has a redeeming influence. And some useful qualities, such as alertness, forethought, patience and judgment, have undoubtedly been developed by it. But its influence on production is to my mind deadly and numbing. To feel that you are working for the market *kills* all interest in your work.

I feel this quite decisively myself. When I am working for *use*, when I am hoeing potatoes and thinking of them only as food—thinking how somebody will eat them, at any rate—and studying how to grow them best for that purpose, then I have an assured good before me which no one can take away. Whatever their *price*, these potatoes will feed the same number of human beings. I feel calm and contentful, and can take pleasure in my work. But when I am working for the market, when the profit and the gain which I am to derive from the sale of my potatoes is the main object before me—when I am considering all along whether each thrust of the hoe will *pay*, whether I had not better scamp this or hurry over that in view of the falling prices, when I see that the whole end and purpose of my labor is involved in doubt owing to trade fluctuations which I cannot possibly foresee—then—(how can it be otherwise?)—I am miserable and feverish, grudging every stroke of the tool in my hand, each effort of the muscles, tossed about by uncertainty, wavering in my plans, and devoid of that good heart which alone is the basis of all good work. Certainly I may be, shall be, longer over my work in the first case than in the second; but I shall produce better stuff—and if I *enjoy* my work I shall not mind an hour additional at it, but if I hate it, *all* the time spent on it is lost. Business conducted on the latter principle may be tolerable, while the prospect of winning draws one on, and before the gambling pleasure has palled, but after that, no! The whole of production to-day is vitiated by the fact that it is production for gain, for profit. There is no assured good in it, no certain advantage or enjoyment in the work—success depends on conditions which are beyond the control of the worker or employer. But it is not wise for anyone to let success depend on things which are beyond his control. The evil principle searches down and affects the lowermost grades of industry, and there is hardly a man nowadays to be found who can be said to be happy in his work. Yet if production were for use, success would be within the reach of everybody. No man, if he only worked for five minutes, need fear that his work will be lost by a fluctuation of the market. No fluctuation of the market will spoil the knife-edge that I have been grinding, nor any change in the price of turnips make these that I am singling less useful for food. My work is secure when I have done it well, and its result is secure—I can whistle and sing at my ease.

Trade is against nature, it is in the long run against human nature, as long as "What can I get?" is its motto. The true nature of man is to give like the son; his getting must be subordinate to that. When giving, his thoughts are on others and he is "free"; when getting, his thoughts are on himself—he is anxious, therefore, and miserable. As long as Trade takes "What can I get?" for its axiom, anxiety and misery will characterise all its work—as they do to-day.

PRIVATE PROPERTY.

"For property alone Law was made."
—*Macaulay.*

"For I will have none who will not open his door to all; treating others as I have treated him.

"The trees that spread their boughs against the evening sky, the marble that I have prepared beforehand these millions of years in the earth, the cattle that roam over the myriad hills—they are Mine, for all my children—

"If thou lay hands on them for thyself alone, thou art accursed."

It is common enough for a large owner—say of land—not to know his own property, certainly not the limits of it, by sight. And it may be asked in what sense such person owns such land.

To own means to confess, to recognise, to acknowledge. A shepherd *owns* his sheep: he knows each one from the others; a man *owns* his neighbor in the street. But this one does not even recognise his land when he sees it. His servants, the common people in his neighborhood, know more about his property than he does.

This may sound strange, but, in fact, I believe there is very little land in this country but what is owned in this sort of way. The legal owner—even if he knows the exact boundaries—knows little really about his property. For all information as to the nature of the soil, the variety of trees and plants which may be found on it, the crops for which it is adapted, the course of water or of stone beneath the surface, and so forth, he has to refer to the common people who are working for him. It is almost certain that he would not recognise a bit of his own soil if it was brought to him, and if by any chance a small portion of the same were to adhere to his hands he would not *own that*, but hastily retreating would wash it off, lest he should appear too familiar with it! While the people about him, and working on the land, are continually thinking (as I have often had occasion to notice) what can be done for the land, how they can best *do justice* to it—spending affection and thought upon it—and indeed grieving when they see it neglected, when they see it undrained or insufficiently manured, or allowed to run to waste and dishevelment—even though these matters are, as the saying is, "not their concern," and make no difference to their pockets: while, I say, the common people spend this love and affection on the land, the legal owner, *as a rule*, is thinking concerning it of only one thing—and that is how much money he can get out of it. (This was not always so markedly the case as it is nowadays, for, at one time, I believe, the landlord was a much more genuine personage.)

The question then is, which is the true owner Is it the man who, spending thought and affection and labor on the land, blesses it with increase, and causes its face to smile with glad produce ? or is it the man who, hardly knowing even the boundaries of

PRIVATE PROPERTY. 141

that which he possesses, and feeling no warming of the heart towards it to make it beautiful and fruitful, thinks only of what advantage he can gain from it, and of how much rent the law will allow him to scrape from its surface?

And what exactly *is* this legal ownership? In the case of land, it is the power to evict, to prosecute for poaching, to levy rent, etc. It is essentially a negative power. It is the power to *prevent others from using*. It is the power to turn all the inhabitants off your land and convert it into a deer forest; or to prevent anyone from tilling any part of your soil. The landlords of England might starve the English people out. The people must pay rent in order to be *allowed* to produce their own food. And so with all property, the legal ownership is essentially negative; it is the power to prevent other people from using. Note well that it is not the power to use the thing yourself. A man may have a fine telescope but be quite incapable of using it; yet he has the legal power to prevent anyone else looking through it. So a man may possess a fine tract of land, and yet be ignorant of agriculture and incapable even of handling a spade; he may not even have the money to set others to work on it; the *law* supplies him with no force or means wherewith to cultivate that land, it merely supplies him if he wishes, with a (police) force to prevent others from using it. And if there are any useful natural products upon or beneath the surface, it enables him to keep them *all to himself*.

It is as well to remember this. Some people think a great deal of law and legal right, and no doubt it is quite proper that they should do so. And indeed it may well be that this kind of thing is necessary at a certain stage of civilisation; but it is as well to remember that it is in itself essentially negative and anti-social. More than that—and flowing from that —I think it may well be seen that *mere* legal ownership is essentially harmful. For it is a great power, and like all great power, if not humanised by loving application it must tend to destruction. The man who has money is like the man who controls the floodgates of an estuary. He can turn the current (which is always flowing) into this channel or that; he can launch the flood in devastation over the lands, or he can bind it in its course to carry the barks of Peace and Plenty along its shores; he can create order and life, or he can precipitate ruin and death. But there is just this difference—that it is easier to destroy than to create, and any random application of wealth—though strictly legal—being merely careless or selfish, is pretty sure to bring ruin and distress with it, whereas it is certain that one must give careful thought to the spending of the same to make it fruitful of order and of joy.

This only illustrates what Ruskin has said, for those who would learn from him, that "wealth is the possession of the valuable by the valiant." Property does not become true *wealth* till it comes into the hands of one who is able and willing to use it well. In the hands of another man it may just as likely be *illth*. Vast tracts of land in the hands of an owner who gives no care or thought to its use, who perhaps does not use it at all in any effective sense, but lives in Paris or London—lands undrained, perhaps, and breeding malaria, or left in the hands of agents whose sole business is to rack-rent the tenants, and so to induce widespread agricultural paralysis—such lands, or rather (since the lands themselves are right enough) the false ownership in them, is *illth*. Buy costly and elaborate dinners, so that you may never know the clean and natural desire for food; buy a carriage, so that you may never have to walk; buy heavy-piled furniture and hangings for your room, so that you may not breathe the fragrant air of heaven, and you will breed disease and death—your wealth will have become illth. And not only for yourself, but—if you follow it out—probably also for those who have to prepare you these things. Use the same money to set twenty honest people to some wholesome and useful work; use it for them freely and friendly and it will buy bread and life,—it will feed their hearts and their bellies both. And not them only, but others whom you cannot see. In the one case your possession will be a nuisance, in the other it will be a blessing. The first course is the easy one—of mere legality; the second is the difficult one—of humanity.

Thus, as a first step towards the subject before us, I think we may fairly make the following general statement, *viz.*, that legal ownership is essentially a negative and anti-social thing; and that, unless qualified or antidoted by human relationship, it is pretty certain to be absolutely *harmful*. In fact, when a man's chief plea is " The law allows it," you may be pretty sure he is up to some mischief!

We may now pass on to a consideration of what property really means. If legal ownership is a negative thing, is there some reality of which it is, as it were, the shadow, which it has at some time or other vainly tried to represent?

In what sense, for instance, can one really own a material object, an animal, or even a man? Let us take the last first. A slave-owner could, by virtue of the law, force a slave to do his will; but there have been many masters who, without application of the law, have been able to get the same result—by personal ascendancy, by the establishment of a sincere relation between themselves and the owned, by affectionate care. In these cases the ownership has been *more* complete, the will more faithfully obeyed, the tie of attachment stronger than chains. This kind of ownership is, at least, nearer the reality than the other.

So with an animal—affection, courage, personal mastery produce the true attachment. The dog runs away from his legal owner to his true owner. In both these cases, property in its reality appears as a *trust*. You are in trust for the creature that you own. To keep a man (slave or servant) for your own advantage merely, to keep an animal that you may *eat* it, is a lie. You cannot look that man or animal in the face. They may be your property according to law, but you have no pleasurable sense of ownership in them, only discomfort.

Now these cases relate to living beings, and what sense of true ownership you have, arises through right relation to those beings. But can you have ownership of inorganic matter—of the mere *materials* of life? Say, can you positively really and truly own a single chemical atom? Can you control, can you command it—and how will you begin? (I do not say that you cannot—on the contrary, I have dreamed that there is an authority over these things, quite similar to, and on the same conditions as the former cases—but that is a kind of authority very little studied at present.) Can you say to the little bit of camphor which you wrap so neatly in paper and put in your drawer, "Little bit of camphor, you are mine," —and in a day or two you open the paper, and lo! there is nothing there? or to the treasures in chest and closet which the moth and the rust are duly and diligently all the while corrupting, "Treasures, treasures, you are all mine, mine, Mine!" Yes, you can say so; but in what sense exactly do you say so? Is it merely in the legal sense that you rub your hands as you gaze bending over them, and say, "I can prevent *anyone else* from using you,"—or is it in a grander sense than this? And if so, in *what* sense?

Can we get anything out of the word Property itself? That which is proper to a thing. What are the properties of brimstone—its essential characteristics, qualities, relations to other things? What is the property of chalk as distinguished from cheese? What are the properties of vegetable life, of animal life? What is the essential Property of Man?

This last is the question of questions. Amid all the shows and illusions, is it possible that the reality which we seek is hidden here? What if material property is only a symbol and indication of it? All the scrambling after calculable wealth, all the delusions and illusions, all the bog-floundering and fatuous wisp-catching are not in vain, if they lead us to find an answer to *that*, if they show us at last the wealth which is truly incalculable.

At any rate I think we can begin to see, in part, that there is a sense in which a man can own material property—more true, more *real*, than the legal sense. I fancy the bread, fragrant and sweet from the baking, which a man eats in peace and thankfulness of heart, becomes his *property*. It passes into his sinews and brain, and serves his will. It becomes his life, and enters, for the time, into faithful obedient relation to *him*. I do not think that the costly food eaten in greediness of spirit becomes his property. I am sure that it torments him a deal, all down those canals and colons, and is not faithful and obedient to his will. Sometimes, indeed, the slave arises and slays him who should have been his master. I fancy that the coat which a man wears in singleness of spirit, and ready if need be to give it to some one who is more in want than himself, becomes, for the time, his *property*. It enters into some beautiful and expressive but indescribable relation to himself, and has more grace than the richest drapery. I fancy that the ground which a man tills and tends with loving care becomes, for the time being, his *property*. It answers to *him*, it becomes one of his qualities. The young trees put forth their leaves gratefully to him, and the furrows shoot rich and green, for he blesses them.

Thus, though we may not have got to the bottom of the matter yet, it does appear that true ownership in man, animal, or material wealth, cannot exist without some living and human relationship to the object owned

Without this relation, ownership is a mere form; it may be legal, but it must be dead, and therefore harmful.

Perhaps the most effective example of this sort of thing is a man's property in the creation of his own hands. This would seem to be the original type of private property. If I cut a stick in the wild woods, whittle it, peel it, polish it, and transform it into a walking-stick, the universal consent of mankind allows me a right in that stick. And why? Because as far as it is a product of anything besides Nature, it is a product of my *work*. I have entered into the closest relationship to it; I have put *myself* into it; it has become part of me—one of my properties.

As the quality of the work rises, as the quantity of good humanity put into it increases—whether in the shape of manual effort, or ingenious thought, or loving artfulness—so does the true *value* of the object increase; and so does the good sense of mankind confirm the right of property in it to the man who thus produced it. A bow and arrows may have more work put into it than a walking-stick; it has more value. A fiddle may have still more. The violins of Stradivari were his property, commercially speaking, before he sold them; but, indeed, he put so much of his self into them that they still, in a sense, belong to him—and to no one else—they are vocal with his presence. And of his great poem, "Leaves of Grass," Whitman says, "Who touches this touches a man." He has fairly passed himself into it, and to such a degree that he and it can never be parted. Types and impressions of the book may be sold, but it remains his splendid property and glorious manifestation to all time.

To keep then to just the ordinary walks of life, we see that creation by his own labor is the most original and indeed valid claim which a man can have to private property in material wealth, and taking all in all—ruffianism duly allowed for—the most widely accepted. When, however, labor becomes more social, and many combine for the production of one thing, a difficulty arises. The product is no longer the creation of one man, but of many; and, as the process becomes more complex, ultimately of *society*. The product, therefore, is—or should be—the property of society. The man is paid in counters or checks, which are called wages, and which represent—or ought to represent—the average human value which he has put into the product. The wages are now his private property. They are not property in so near and personal a sense as the walking-stick, or the bow and arrows; but from that personal relationship to one object, which he had before, he has now exchanged into a social relationship; and, having given so much human value to society, he can now have its equivalent back again in any form that he pleases. He has lost in intensity of personal ownership, but he has gained in breadth and variety of command.

Thus we have a second stage of private property when it becomes social. The human value put into an object does not come back to the man *in* that object, but it comes back to him in counters or checks, that is in *money*, transmutable into human values in all sorts of objects. But here we come upon a difficulty which is a very serious one—in fact, quite insurmountable—the crux and the sphinx-riddle of all political and social economy, namely, how can we reduce the work of one man and the work of another to one standard? What is the measure of human value, and therefore of all value? There is, of course, no answer to this. That is, there *is* an answer, but it does not admit of being formulated in words; the progress of society itself through the ages is the process by which the answer is being slowly ground out. From time to time temporary answers are given, as for instance, "The value of an object is what it will fetch in the market," or "The value of an object is proportional to the number of hours of human labor embodied in it," and though one such answer may be an improvement on another, it is clear that none may stand the criticism of time—and that the successive social systems founded on them are from the outset doomed to destruction—till the millennium is reached —when society, we suppose, will accept no formulated measures or laws, but will be ruled from within.

Despite, however, this huge difficulty in the theory of value, which thus affects collaterally any definition of private property in its social aspect, let us cheerfully push on a little farther.

We have said that if there is to be any distinction between property in its merely legal sense, and in its true sense, the distinction must reside in the living and human relation involved in the latter as opposed to the former. But we see also that in the second or social stage of property the relationship to the product of your own labor is weakened. A man instead of having a good yew bow as the product of his day's work has 5s. This is a decided falling off—a few counters instead of the sturdy product of his own thought and toil. What sentiment can he have for his own five shillings more than for his neighbor's? What *private* property in them, except in the barest legal sense? But this sad relapse is partly made good when he comes to use his counters. With his five shillings say he buys a spade. Then this spade—though not the product of his toil—represents indirectly such a product; and as he comes to *use* the spade day after day, gradually he restores the lost sense of personal relationship—the spade grows to his hand, and at length it becomes his very own, a prolongation of himself, his property in the most effective and intimate sense.

Thus we have property arising first from individual creation, then passing through the generalised form of Money, or exchange, and finally regaining its personal and private sanction in use.

Use then is an important element in the definition of true property. This is clear enough. If I accumulate counters as the product of my toil, the objects for which I finally exchange those counters will be—or should be—my property. But if with those counters I buy a horse, which kicks me off its back, and continues kicking me off, then clearly I have lost my property! True, I may still have legal property in it—I may still be able to prevent others from using it—but I shall have no true enjoyment or possession, since I cannot use it myself. Or to take the example given by Ruskin: the man on board ship who tied his gold in a belt round his waist to make it secure, *thought* that that gold was his property; but when the ship capsized and he was in the water he saw that he was mistaken; he found that he was the property of the gold, for it took him to the bottom. In order for true ownership, there must be *use*, which means *mastery*, which means exercise of *will*, of human power. Every object is a challenge to our manhood—till we have mastered it—taken possession of it; and it is only "ours" when we have put forth our living power upon it.

As an example of use, of mastery: I knew a coachman who was devoted to his master's horses. When he came into the stable the horses would purr and whinny with delight, kissing him as he went up to them in their stalls. That man could do anything with those horses. The Stock Exchange magnate who was driven behind them to the station each day knew little and cared less about them. He was the legal owner, but the other surely was the true owner. Even the powers of the legal owners are limited in these cases. It is in vain that the young lord says that he will take such-and-such a horse out hunting, if the groom has determined that he shall not; the latter can invent a score of good reasons to gain his point, which the former cannot gainsay. The garden practically belongs to the gardener; it is he who determines what flowers shall be cut, what seeds shall be sown; and it is a common remark that the servants are the rulers of our large domestic establishments—and just, because authority is the natural result of labor, whether in production or in use.

The money form of property is, as I have said, that

in which there is least of the personal and human element, and so it comes about that the stage of civilisation in which money is most sought after is just that in which though there is most worship of private property there is least realisation of the same in any true sense. To this stage belongs the mania for accumulation. Money becomes an end in itself, apart from all noble and joyful sense of mastery; and material objects represent money, instead of money representing them. Instead of wealth consisting in mastery, it comes to consist in the number of objects to be mastered—a pretty quandary! The unfortunate man who is beset by this mania can rest no more. He lays field to field and house to house; he buys books, dress, variety of food, drink, entertainment—each time thinking now he will be satisfied. And each time finding out his mistake, he presses forward another step in the same direction (*i.e.*, farther from the ultimate goal). As James Hinton says, "We are like children who eat, and eat, and eat, ignorant that food is for nutrition." The children have mistaken the object of food, so we of property.

Food is for nutrition, not for gratification of the sense of taste, nor for accumulation in the bowels. It nourishes the body in passing through it. So of property: it is not for gratification of the sense of ownership, nor for accumulation in strong boxes, store-rooms, and old stockings, that it exists. The moment it begins to accumulate disease sets in. "Lay not up for yourselves treasures upon earth, where moth and rust doth corrupt, and where thieves break through and steal."

Man is like a flame—which shines by virtue of the current of materials passing through it. Check that current, and his brightness will be materially diminished; let the products of combustion accumulate if but a few moments, and his light will be extinguished. Use and pass on, use and pass on—that is the word, and admit no more than you can use.

Go into grand houses. What are these books rotting by hundreds on the library shelves, these boudoirs and best rooms seldom opened, with fusty smelling furniture, these forgotten dresses lying in the deeps of unexplored wardrobes? What are these accumulations of money, of certificates and securities, of jewels and of plate, hoarded away in safes and strong boxes and at the bank? They are the signs of disease. They are similar to the accumulations of fat in an over-corpulent person, of smoke and soot in an ill-regulated flame. They mar the beauty, the grace, the dignity, and the power of man. Of disease, remember, for when did you ever meet an owner of this sort who was at ease—as your dog lying on the hearth-rug is at ease, though it owns nothing? England is full of such undigested wealth; she is congested, sick, sick almost to death with it. And while her upper classes are suffering a chronic indigestion from this accumulation of dead matter upon them, while they are rendered imbecile, diseased, and absolutely pestilent by it, her poor are dying for mere want of nourishment.

Thus once more we come to the necessity of use as a justification of possession; but this opens up a further and final question, namely, that of *right* use.

It is obvious that we cannot allow a man property in a horse, however often or however well he may ride it, if he uses it to run down old women and children in the street. We take the knife away from the child because it cannot use it rightly; and so the good sense of mankind takes away even the product of his own labor from the man who is going to damage others with it. Society puts forward a claim to over-rule the individual in this matter. But it does not tell us what right use is, nor am I going to attempt a definition. We have to work out these things by degrees. All considerations—the slow progress of society, the successive attempts of law to come to a satisfactory definition of the rights of property, and its continual failure, all point to the fact that, until the individual and society are properly harmonised, property cannot be rightly held. It is only when a man enters into the region of equality that a solution offers itself. In finding the true Property of Man he finds the secret of all ownership; and in surrendering all rights of private property, and accepting poverty, he really becomes possessor of all social wealth, and, for the first time, infinitely rich.

And now a few words in a historical sense. Private property, as a legal right, has not always existed in the past, and will not always in the future. There will come a time in the future, as there has been in the past, when *law* will have nothing at all to say on this subject. It has now in fact become abundantly clear from late researches that in a certain early stage of history Man passes through a phase of communism. Columbus in one of his letters mentions with regard to some West

Indian tribes, at the time of his discovery, that they appeared to hold things in common. A traveller, lately writing home, says that he tried to explain to one of the Samoan Islanders of the Pacific the system that prevails in Great Britain and other civilised countries—how some people were rich while others were poor—and that oftentimes one man would be actually starving, while another would have more bread than he could eat; but he, the wretched islander—being used to a communistic state of society—*could not understand* the possibility of such a situation; his poor heathen brain was positively unequal to the task of comprehending the glorious blessings of our Christian civilisation.

In an early phase of history, then, when men go in tribes or clans cemented by blood-relationship, the desire for private property is weak. The clan has property, but the individual hardly any. In this stage of society, as would appear from various circumstances, the individual self is to a large extent lost or fused in the tribal self. The man owns, but owns *in common* with his mates (the same may be seen in ants or bees). He fights fiercely with those of another clan, and will seize *their* goods for the benefit of his own side, or kill *them*; but to quarrel with, or steal from, or injure one of his own people is exceedingly rare—rarer (as I think all observers agree) than in our more civilised countries. His self is almost one with the tribal self.

Later on comes this individualising of self, and this accentuation of private property; and a huge, elaborate, and in the present day cumbrous and collapsing, system of laws arises for the purpose of defining these individual rights, and the limits of property. What is the meaning of this vast fungus-growth which has overshadowed civilisation so long? It is obvious that it must have had some purpose, some function, in the history of our race.

I take it that it is a part of the development of man. I take it that it is necessary that the individual should be excluded from the tribe (as the child is excluded from its mother's womb) that he may learn the lessons of individuality; that he may learn his powers, and the mastery over things; that he may learn his right relations to others, and the misery of mere self-seeking and individual greed; and that having learned these lessons, and so to speak found the limits of Self, he may once more fuse that Self—not now again with the tribe, but with something greater and grander, namely Humanity.

Of this process, then, of the development of the individual, the institution of private property has, I take it, been the great engine. Growing up from small beginnings, it has gradually had the effect of separating each individual man from the community of his fellows; it has raised a kind of artificial wall or barrier between. Acting on his specially selfish instincts, it has drawn these out to a degree probably unprecedented before in the history of his race; but the compensation has been that in this isolation it has developed in man a certain growth in the sense of individuality—which was necessary and which would have been impossible without it. Within this network, this honeycomb, this penitentiary of laws and institutions connected with private property, each individual as in a separate cell, with much tribulation, has learned or is learning these lessons. When they are learnt, the need of the barriers and the cells will disappear; and, slowly and gradually, as it came, the institution of private property will pass away.

If I have said anything, therefore, or been understood to say anything, against property—legal property—I recant it. It is a step, a necessary step, in human development; like many other things it is an illusion, but it is also an indication. Man rising from the savage state, reaching as it were his majority, comes into property (especially is this true of the present day with its vast accessions of material power and wealth), and doesn't know what on earth to do with it! He hasn't an idea of its uses. He hoards it, he hides it, he pursues it, he dances round it, hugs it, kisses it, puts it on his head, his back, circles his arms, his fingers with it—falls down and worships it. He locks it in a box and lies awake at night thinking of it; he conceals it in his mattress; he buries it in a bank—as a dog does a bone—and presently the bank grows so big that it has to have columns and a portico; he prowls about the shop windows, staring at it through panes of glass; he buys revolvers and policemen to defend it, and dresses people like himself up in wigs and gowns to talk wise about it—and then believes what they say. He behaves in fact like a madman, and hasn't an idea what he is doing. But there is a method in his madness nevertheless. He thinks that by all these antics he is really getting at something substantial—and so in a sense he is. He is finding out his *own* properties, he is learning to possess himself.

The material property which he is pursuing is an illusion. It serves its purpose for a time. He is very tenacious of it at first; it exercises him dreadfully, and he flies into violent tempers over it. But by the time he has learned to control these little passions it seems to have lost some of its attraction! In the beginning he is a great stickler for his rights over it, and goes to law considerably, but in the end he is glad to get done with it and the whole blessed tranclament of cares and anxieties connected with it.

Money may be gain, and it may be power; but it is not always either to him who has it. More properly, it is the symbol of a Gain, which he may attain to—it is the symbol of a Power, which lies within him. When the realities are seized, the symbol will drop off as useless—or be only used *as* a symbol. When a man has learned whose superscription there is on the coin he uses, he has learned everlasting life.

To return to the historical clue: the practical advantages which money gives in the present day— such as travel, art, books, leisure—must not be ignored or undervalued. They are all part of education and development, and are valuable at a certain stage. But as society progresses, and emerges from the child state, even these values of private riches tend to become daily less. Art galleries, free libraries, and the solution of the industrial problem will provide everybody with the three last; travel is already marvellously cheap, and will become cheaper. Before so very long the need and the use of private property will disappear from social life. It will figure only as an encumbrance; law, as I have said, will cease to take any cognisance of its existence; and the curve of progress will bring us back to the communism of early society on another and higher plane of human development.

The problem of life is ultimately extraordinarily simple; and when society has recovered from the daze and nightmare which oppresses it, and has reestablished the simple honest relation between man and man, it will be seen to be so. All the problems of society depend ultimately on the problem of the individual's own life. All questions of material property come back ultimately, as already hinted, to the question, What is the true relation of Man to material things? When the key to that has been found, all these other difficulties vanish entirely—like a flake of snow touched by a drop of water. They disappear and exist no more. The questions of food, clothing, housing, literature, etc., will not then need to give anyone a moment's anxiety. As to travelling, "it is not worth while," as Thoreau says, "to go round the world in order to count the cats in Zanzibar." If you do not happen to have the means to go to Brazil, set out travelling to Heaven. It is a longer journey, and you will see more by the way. Nay, I would say to the wealthy, travel in your own township. Put off your fine clothes and go among the poor and oppressed; work at the bench with the carpenter's son, and in the pit with the collier; go on the road with the tramp and lighten the way a little for his feet—and you will hear things you never thought to have heard, you will see things that in all your grand tours you could never attain to see.

Like other problems, the problem of property is best solved indirectly. That is, not by seeking material wealth directly, but by seeking that of which material wealth is only the symbol. "Seek ye first the kingdom . . . . and all these things shall be added unto you."

Vaguely metaphorical as these words sound, yet I believe they express a literal fact. To this generation, weary with worshiping its gold and silver, its steam-engines and its commerce, seeking first its dependence on instead of its kingdom over material things, they express the fact that not in this way can it gain what it seeks. Its idols are dead; for all the worship that is rendered to them they grant nothing in return. The quest is illusive. Seeking ease we have found disease; scrambling for wealth our civilisation has become poverty-stricken beyond all expression; prizing mere technical knowledge we have forgotten the existence of wisdom; and setting up material property as our deity we have dethroned the ruling power in our own natures. Not till this last is restored can we possibly attain to possession of the other things. Materials are not to be worshiped—they must be commanded. Nature is one; she is loyal to herself from the centre to the very circumference. Till you have established a right relation with that centre, till you have loyally sought and found within yourself the password, do not think she will be such a fool as to surrender to you her outposts. On the contrary, till such time, she will taunt and deride you; she will tantalise you with shadows and mock you with illusions of gain—but in reality you will have nothing, enjoy nothing, nor be capable of owning anything.

Finally, and lest we should wander away into mere abstractions and generalisations, let us try and apply some of our principles to practice. It seems to me that the principles which I have sought to establish *are* eminently practical. I have tried to show that wealth, in order really to *be* wealth, must be humanised. Mere legal possession is nothing, or worse than nothing; it is an injury to the community. This is, alas! only too well illustrated in our modern society. The wealth of the wealthy is for the most part a dead inhuman wealth—a corruption—a mortification. The land is not owned in any true sense, it is left in the hands of agents and stewards, who must, from the nature of the case, act on a rule of inhumanity. The great industries are not owned in any true sense, but the shareholders and bondholders to whom they legally belong live ignorant even of the nature of their possessions, and leave directors and managers to screw down their workmen—satisfied so long as they provide the usual dividend at the end of the half year. What we have to do—what society has to do—is to divide this false ownership from the true ownership, and cast it out; and that quickly, for already the process of mortification is far gone, and only a serious operation can avert death. We must say to the landholders of this and other countries, "Unless you put your lands to some human use, unless you hold them in trust for the good of the people, we shall take them from you—and that quickly—for by every acre that you are now devoting to your own aggrandisement merely you are murdering a brother." To the man who now owns ten farms, we may fairly say, "If you like to go and live on one of your farms to till and tend it, well and good; do so by all means; that is true ownership. But the ownership you have in the other nine farms is a mere legal ownership; you cannot till and tend them too; all you are doing with them is to 'prevent others from using them' by your system of private rents. Here your ownership is absolutely harmful, so without more ado, clear out!"

And to the shareholders and bondholders of this and other countries we may fairly say, "What are you doing with your properties? Have you any human relation to them at all? Do you come together at your meetings to consider how best to administer them for the public good, how to turn out the usefullest and most genuine articles, how to compass the welfare of the men engaged in them? If not, then you are doing nothing, and worse than nothing with them—you are using your legal power to aggrandise yourselves, to enrich yourselves at the cost of these others, you are by just so much preventing others from the use of these properties, you are by just so much strangling the natural life of the people—begone! the whole pack of you, and let us never see your faces again!"

Clearly the sooner we get rid of all mere law in the matter of property the better. The good sense of mankind, as I have already said, will always allow a man his claim in the product of his own hands, or his own labor; and the same good sense will never dispute a man's right in that which he puts to good human use. These may safely be left to the unwritten law of all ages. Whatever is not of these is of the devil. The claims which people put in for wealth for which they never labored, the rights which they assume in property which they use to degrade others with, are of the devil. And these are the claims and the rights which written and printed laws are specially constructed to secure. It must be one of our most practical objects to break down by degrees this whole apparatus of chicanery; and so at length to *free* true property from the vast accumulations of false ownership which in later times have so disguised the reality that we hardly any longer know what it is.

Many immediate applications might be made of the principles which we have indicated. Thus not only, as we have said, might ownership in land be at once limited to *occupying* ownership, but the same principle might be (more roughly) applied to personal property. We might, I mean, at once and as a first approximation, say that no one could fairly and humanly use an income of over £5,000 a year (I should not like myself to have to use a tenth part of it) and so by cumulative or prohibitive taxation transfer at once a large quantity of idle and dead wealth into the occupancy of the people for living and public uses. And I maintain that such measures as these are in the highest degree practical, simply because they involve a question of life and death to the nation. England and indeed all "civilised" countries to-day are simply in advanced stages of mortification. The accumulation of dead matter upon them is such that if it continues to take place much longer the organism as a whole must inevitably perish. The belt of gold is taking us swiftly and surely to the bottom. Nothing but a vitalising of the national possessions by use—use *by* the people, and *for* the people—can save us, and already even for that the time is short.

So true is it that the moral and ultra-moral laws penetrate right down into the concerns of ordinary life. Far and away up beyond all our theories and definitions stands the true Manhood—the real Property of Man—of which the other is only the sign and emblem. Are we true to that invisible point, that inward polestar of our human nature—are we masters of wealth in that invisible region?—then we descend with authority upon outward possessions to master them, and our national life is sane and prosperous; but without such radiation from within all our gold is simply ashes.

To build up this Supreme Life in a people—the life of Equality—in which each individual passes out of himself along the lives of his fellows, and in return receives their life into himself with such force that he becomes far greater as an individual than ever before—partaker of the supreme power, and well-nigh irresistible—to build up this life in a people may well be a task worthy of the combined efforts of poets, philosophers, and statesmen. The whole of history and all the age-long struggles of the nations point to this realisation. Even now society like a chrysalis writhes in the birth-throes of the winged creature within. Equality—the vanishing of the centuries-long conflict between the individual and his fellows—the attainment by each man of a point where all this war of interests ceases to exist, and the barriers which divide man from man are thrown down—this is, indeed, that Freedom for which all of history has been one long struggle and preparation. No mere outward equality, no monotony of external condition—far from it—but the equality of the "members of the body" fulfilling their various functions in perfect inward harmony. This state of society, the ideal and the dream of so many ages, is after all not so impossible of realisation, not so very extravagant. If a single healthy human or animal body exists, surely a healthy human society may exist. In the backward past, in the early communal life to which we have alluded, this state of society has existed in its embryonic or seed-like form, and when the immense nightmare of what we call civilisation, when the long period of growing pains and bitter negative experience which we are now going through has passed away, it will exist again in its glorified and universal form. The morning stars will once more sing together, and exiled man will re-enter the gates which the flaming sword so long has guarded.

THE ENCHANTED THICKET.

"And the thorns sprang up and choked them."

In gathering together the foregoing papers into one volume I would fain say a last word by way of appeal to you, the specially wealthy and respectable classes. The situation is so grave, the crisis hastens so, all over the civilised world. What are you going to do? What part are you going to play in the great drama on which the curtain is just rising?

As one walks through the vast polite wildernesses of the West End of London, and the endless suburban villa-regions of all our great towns—in extent and wealth and standard of luxury visibly and rapidly increasing from year to year—as one sips one's tea in the drawing-room, or listens to the after-dinner conversation over the wine and walnuts, there steals upon one I know not what sense of antediluvian slumber, of strange and may be fatal lethargy. All is so elegant, so easy, so finished—one dreams on as in an enchanted palace, and the noise of the actual world dies out at last from one's ears. And yet, when a man comes to look into it, he sees that it is just here, in these enchanted palaces, that the danger and the disease of modern society lies. He cannot help feeling that these who live here are really, as William Morris calls them, the *dangerous classes*—

not the poor half-starved wretches, puny and stunted in person, and empty in purse, who, mad with rage, are belched forth in their thousands and hundreds of thousands from the slums of our great cities—not these, terrible as they are, are the real danger. They are only the reaction, the protest, the necessary outcome, and perhaps, after all, the hopeful ending of a great wrong. It is in these great clotted and congested centres which call themselves "society," but through which the true life-blood of society does *not* circulate—in the slow poison and paralysis of the life there—in the fatal mortification of these centres which, with their vast wealth and influence, spread claws of contagion all through the vital organism in which they occur, that the serious peril lies, which perhaps only a serious convulsion may avert.

In truth the very extent of these congested regions is already a difficulty. For they are so vast that you who live within them have hardly a chance to know what is going on in the real world. The cry of the starving children, the price of whose maintenance for a week is consumed by you in a single ordinary meal, reaches not your ears. It has too far to travel. Sometimes, indeed, a tale of suffering may penetrate, but it sounds far off like a dream. How can you do anything? A thousand shackles, worse than any tangled thicket, have grown up round the sleeping soul.

You sit in rooms crowded with knick-knacks, elegant trifles from all parts of the world. They are interesting; I have not a word to say against them. And in the next house the rooms are crowded with similar trifles, and in the next, and the next; and for miles round the same. The servants have to dust them every day, the owners never look at them—hardly know what they are. For whom do they exist? If in a plainly furnished cottage one such thing were seen, it would actually be examined—it would be a delight, a real curiosity, a bright suggestion of form and color, an adornment of work-a-day life; but here it is so gratuitously useless that it enfeebles the mind that gazes on it; it is no adornment, for there is no real life to adorn.

It is all congestion. Congestion at the dance—so many people, such dresses, that dancing is impossible. Congestion at the dinner-party—congestion in twelve courses; so much to eat that eating is impossible. Congestion of books—so much to read, that reading is impossible. Congestion in church—stitched and starched up to the eyes (while the servants at home are preparing the roast beef and plum pudding). Congestion at the theatre, at the concert, yawning in dress-clothes on the front seats; while the real enjoyers and observers are out of sight behind. Such a congestion of unused wealth and property, such a glut, as surely the world before has never seen, and to purge which away will surely require such medicine as the world before has never taken—no gilded pill or silent perambulator this time, but a drastic bolus plowing its way through the very frame of "society," not without groans and horrible noises.

And through this maze of congested life—of interests which have ceased to be interesting, of enjoyments which have become bores—to pick the way, what an art it has become! Visitors call in the afternoon, and visits have to be made. The long day has to be eked out—now a cup of tea, now a five-course meal, now a little coffee, and now a turn at the piano. (And all the time what poor girls are pining, what mothers are dying for want of a little help, a little sympathy!) And ever the smallest crumbs of incident to be worked up into "conversation." Some get quite clever at this. They always say the right thing at the right time, are sympathetic, bright, entertaining. Yes—while Nero is fiddling, Rome is burning. Have you no other use for that sensitive heart, that ready tongue, which Nature has given you, than to perpetuate this Fool's Paradise of polite trifling?

A Paradise truly! The hot water arrives so punctually at the bedroom door, the carpets are so soft and warm, the spoons so bright and clean—surely there can't be much amiss in the world! If only these demagogues would keep quiet, these few crack-brained Carlyles and Ruskins—and the faint wolf-howling there far down in the conscience!

Do you not attend church on Sunday, and are you not very philanthropic? Do you not tell each other sad stories about the poor over your ice-pudding, till your lips are pursed with pity? (or is it the pudding?) Do you not undertake excursions to the East End, and get deeply interested in the general question of slums? Is it not all very nice, and just as it ought to be, and wouldn't the poor soon get their wrongs redressed if, instead of naughtily rioting, they were to wait for you to come in your fur cloaks like good fairies, and turn their wretched dens into pleasant palaces?

And yesterday a woman that I know died—died washing—washing rich folks' clothes—at sixpence a dozen! Sixpence a dozen all round—mark that!—a halfpenny each. Not many handkerchiefs and collars when its "all round"—mostly shirts and big things. "It seems a many times passing through your hands even for a penny each," as one in the same line of life said to me—"two rubbings, dollying, two rinsings, wringing, putting out to dry, taking down, folding, mangling, starching and ironing each thing."

It was a good thing, wasn't it, that she died quietly, poor thing, so gentle and loving—without any fuss or rioting in the streets or making comfortable people uncomfortable? Of course *our* clothes are not washed at that price—no blood on them. We all know that. At any rate, we pay fair enough; if the people whom we employ put the washing out on scandalous terms, that is their fault, not ours. We have so many things to attend to, so many big philanthropic schemes, we can hardly be expected to know all about our laundress!

And to-day a hundred porters and signalmen have been discharged from one of the large railways, so as to effect a saving of £5000 a year in expenses! (See note p. 36.) It would have been a pity, wouldn't it, to reduce the dividend in order to save those hundred good industrious folk and their families from being turned into the streets? The diminution of dividend would have very nearly amounted to twopence halfpenny (this is a fact) on every £100 share. Think of that! Twopence halfpenny! It was a good thing those hundred families were turned off, or you might have actually had to go short of a box of chocolate next Christmas!

Is there no sense of sympathy, of responsibility, of mere duty even, in these matters? Has the cry of Cain, "Am I my brother's keeper?" become stereotyped upon the lips of the wealthy? When the shareholder comes for his dividend, when the bondholder comes for his bond, is it nothing to him that human flesh has to submit to the knife in the process, as long as he gets what the law allows him to claim? Is all humanity dead out of the world, and are you rich going to continue for ever this practice of living out of the degradation and death of the poor, which has already become so familiar to you that it seems the most natural thing possible?

And yet after all has been said, do I not know well enough the tender heart that beats within you—for all that the enchanted thicket has grown so strong and tall? You men of the upper classes—numbers of you—so devoted, chivalrous, honorable, attending to the welfare of servants and dependents, conscientious on committees, indefatigable in generosity towards the needy, fairly perplexed night and day in the study how best to distribute your wealth; yet has it never occurred to you that it would be better once for all to abandon this everlasting game of robbing Peter to pay Paul—this Sisyphus labor, this rolling of stones uphill only that they may roll down again? What a relief surely it would be! Here on the one hand, with infinite labor in your profession, with infinite care and anxiety in your trade, with infinite trouble even in keeping account of all your rents and dividends, are you gathering a heap together—only to cause yourself fresh labor, fresh anxiety and care in distributing it again, perhaps to the very people you got it from. Why not save this double labor from the beginning? Let the two minuses obliterate each other, and make once more a plus in your life. Here is a circular lying on my table addressed to railway shareholders, and asking subscriptions for a benefit society for the men. What is the good of my first taking a part of their earnings from the men, and then giving the same back to them in a benefit society? What is the good of first depriving the people at large of the means of clothing and feeding themselves, and then coming back to them with clothing clubs and soup kitchens? What is the good of forcing them to work for me under filthy and harmful conditions, and then building hospitals to cure them of the diseases and injuries that I have caused? I might have saved myself the trouble and them the insult. Or do we of the upper classes constitute such a special providence in relation to the working masses that unless their means of livelihood all passed through our hands it would not get properly distributed? You men—educated men as you purport to be—surely you must see the contradiction which is involved in your mode of life, the absurdity! If, above all things, you are practical, do not let this waste and misapplication of your social effort continue.

And you, women of the same class, who have such

capacities of love and sympathy—this life that you lead, with its perpetual denial of humanity, cannot satisfy you for long. You mothers! we plead for the thousands of mothers who, loving their children like you, have to see the little things almost starving before their eyes. You young women! think of the girls in back courts and alleys, or even in rude country villages or mining districts—gentle creatures full of capacities for gaiety, romance, beauty, like yourselves, but too soon to be hardened into spiritless drudges—think! to know you, to have you for a friend, would be a dream of splendor. How much you might give if you would only come nearer these! Think! if you only lived in a place where these could run in and out freely without fear—some simple little cot, where the tide of humanity would wash right up to the door! How they would love you! How that bright gift of tact and sympathy would cheer them! How your ornaments and acquisitions would then become real adornments and curiosities! How you could find a hundred uses for them, and for your books which now lie congested on your shelves! What a busy life—how much of interest, possibly even of love! But now you are shut away—you are in prison. An impenetrable *chevaux de frise* of aimless, heartless, conventionalities and luxuries forbid the entrance of any natural human being. The child of drunken parents may be driven out into the street—but it will not come to you for a refuge No little naked feet will stain your carpet with sacred dirt! The young girl, pure-minded as yourself, but unable to bear the sight of her poverty-stricken parents, may be driven too into the street—but remember that in the hour of her despair she will not come to you; she will not open her heart to you whose fingers are loaded with rings and who have as many dresses as a fancy-woman!—for how should she suppose that you will understand? These high walls, these damask curtains round the windows, these retinues of servants, how shall she penetrate through them to you?

The hedge is growing thicker, my child, thicker and taller round you, and your soul sleeps within.

Ah! I know how your heart bleeds in silence over these things—how you curse the fate which brought you into this world. But how can you move? A thousand chains detain you; round you in every direction stretches the web of polite society—attractive, certainly, in some respects, but oh! how poisonous and paralysing! In this you were born; every fibre of it has entered into your body—how can you escape from it?

The large mirror stands on the toilet-table, and another still larger on the floor. Wherever you look it is only yourself that you see! The servants study your convenience—these wardrobes and chests, they are all for *your* dresses. You who have so desired to give yourself to others, whose loving heart has so yearned to pour itself out, to lose itself, forget itself altogether in others—you are chained to the dead body of yourself! This weary weight you drag from room to room, you cannot escape from it—at the dance, at the concert, it is there! Men smirk round it; servants offer it every attention; but you, the living soul, who would gladly go on your knees and scrub the floor for the feet that you love—hold! Do nothing of the kind, for that would be highly vulgar!

Oh! it is hateful, it is intolerable! Take a torch and go right down to the basement . . . .

No, well do not do that; for after all even a desirable mansion may come in useful for some purpose. But you, if any way possible, clear out of it, your place is not here, and between these walls built on the despair and degradation of others, you will find it as hard to lead a true life as it is "for a camel to go through the eye of a needle."

The evil base of our society eats right through. That our wealthy homes are founded on the spoliation of the poor vitiates all the life that goes on within them. Somehow or other it searches through and degrades the art, manners, dress, good taste of the inmates. While there is time, and before the day of reckoning comes—before the fountains of the great deep are broken up in our vast cities, and chaos horrible ensues—let us hope that some, at least, of these classes will awake from the fatal slumber which enthrals them—a true awakening, no mere uneasy stretching and turning to sleep again. Through the tangled thicket there is but one deliverer that can make his way, and as of old his name is the Prince of Love.

In conclusion, and to look at the matter quite practically, there seems but one immediate step that the wealthy despoiler can take—which at the same time is a most obvious step—and that is, at once or as soon as ever he can, to place his life on the very simplest footing. And this for several reasons. First, because if he must live by other people's labor—and in some cases doubtless his "education" will leave him no other alternative—it is clearly his duty to consume as little of that commodity as he possibly can—(and anyhow experience shows that it is impossible to live very luxuriously on one's own labor alone). Secondly, because only by living simply—that is, on a level of simplicity at least equal to that of the mass of the people—is it possible to know the people, to become friends with them, to gauge their wants, etc.; and here I may say that I do not see that it is the least necessary for a well-to-do person to trouble himself or herself about big philanthropic schemes, or even to join committees of any kind (unless having a special turn that way)—if such an one will only go and live quite quietly in town or country in such an unpretending manner that all, even the poorest, will have ready access without shame, he (or she) will soon find plenty of use for their surplus, and with a certainty of not being imposed upon which they cannot possibly have under other circumstances. Thirdly, because by such a natural life the cares and anxieties of a luxurious household—the innumerable fidgets and worries and obstacles to all true life, together with the dread about being able to maintain it all in the future—are once and for all got rid of. A great load drops off, and the Rubicon once crossed, the difficulties attending the change are seen to be nothing compared with the increased happiness which it brings. Fourthly, because it is only on the knowledge and habits gained in a hardy self-supporting life that the higher knowledge and the fine arts are really founded, and it is as impossible for a statesman to look after a nation properly unless he is acquainted with the first elements of social life, as it is for an artist to paint properly who does not realise the value of homely details, or for a capitalist to do justice to his works and workmen who is ignorant (as is commonly the case nowadays) of the rudiments of the industry which he professes to organise.

And so on. In every department, of morality, good taste, common-sense, private and public expediency, a change in the lives of the rich is called for. It is not necessary to know or to argue about all the changes that will follow. This first step is obvious, and if you take that, the next will become clearer.

THE END.

Printed in Great Britain by Turnbull & Spears, Edinburgh

EDWARD CARPENTER'S WORKS

My Days and Dreams: Being Autobiographical Notes.
Illustrated. Second Edition. Demy 8vo, 7s. 6d. net.

Towards Democracy: Complete Poems. 15th Thousand.
Library Ed., 6s. net; Pocket Ed., 4s. 6d. net.

Towards Industrial Freedom. Cr. 8vo, cloth, 3s. 6d. net;
paper, 2s. 6d. net.

England's Ideal, and other Papers on Social Subjects.
Thirteenth Thousand. Cloth, 3s. 6d. net; limp cloth, 2s. 6d. net.

Civilisation: Its Cause and Cure. 3s. 6d. net and 2s. 6d. net.

Love's Coming-of-Age. 14th Thousand. 3s. 6d. net.

The Intermediate Sex. Crown 8vo, 3s. 6d. net.

Angels' Wings: Essays on Art and Life. 4s. 6d. net.

From Adam's Peak to Elephanta: Sketches in Ceylon and
India. Illustrated. Third Edition. Demy 8vo, cloth, 4s. 6d. net.

A Visit to a Gñani: Four chapters from the above. 1s. 6d. net.

The Promised Land: A Drama. 2s. 6d. net.

Anthology of Friendship (Iolāus). 3s. net.

Chants of Labour: A Song-Book for the People. 1s. net.

The Art of Creation. Third Edition. Cloth, 3s. 6d. net.

Days with Walt Whitman. Crown 8vo, cloth, 4s. 6d. net.

The Drama of Love and Death. Crown 8vo, 5s. net.

Intermediate Types among Primitive Folk. 4s. 6d. net.

The Healing of Nations. Cloth, 3s. 6d. net; paper, 2s. 6d. net.

The Simplification of Life. New Edition. Cr. 8vo, 2s. net.

British Aristocracy and the House of Lords. 6d. net.

Edward Carpenter: The Man and His Message. Pamphlet
by TOM SWAN, with two portraits and copious extracts. 6d. net.

Photogravure Portrait of E. C., with a facsimile autograph,
by MATTISON, 1913. Size 8 × 5½, on Mount 12½ × 10. 2s. 6d. net;
post free 2s. 8d.